ESTATE PU

GRIMSBY · CLE

IMMINGHAM · HOLTON LE CLAY · H

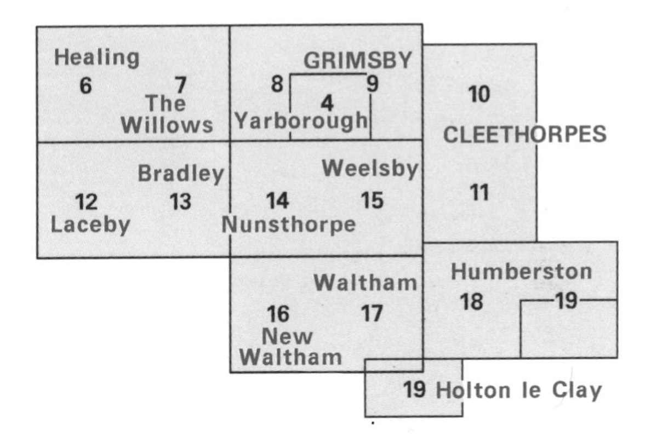

ROAD MAP pages 2-3

ENLARGED CENTRE page 4

INDEX TO STREETS pages 20-24

Every effort has been made to verify the accuracy of information in this book but the publishers cannot accept responsibility for expense or loss caused by an error or omission. Information that will be of assistance to the user of the maps will be welcomed.

The representation on these maps of a road, track or path is no evidence of the existence of a right of way.

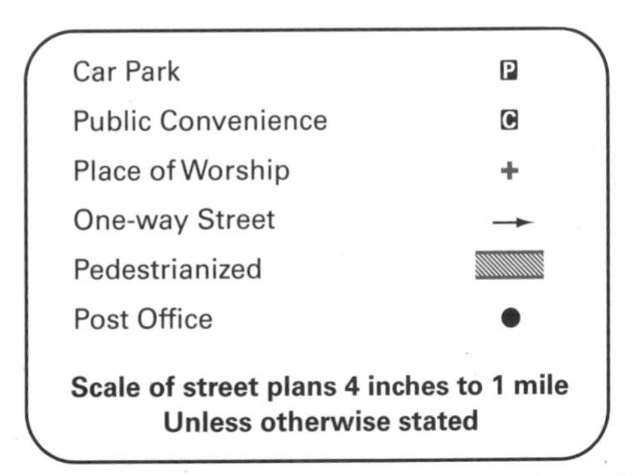

Street plans prepared and published by ESTATE PUBLICATIONS, Bridewell House, TENTERDEN, KENT.
The Publishers acknowledge the co-operation of the local authorities of towns represented in this atlas.

Ordnance Survey® This product includes mapping data licensed from Ordnance Survey® with the permission of the Controller of Her Majesty's Stationery Office.

ISBN 1 84192 077 0

2 ROAD MAP

Scale 3 miles to 1 inch

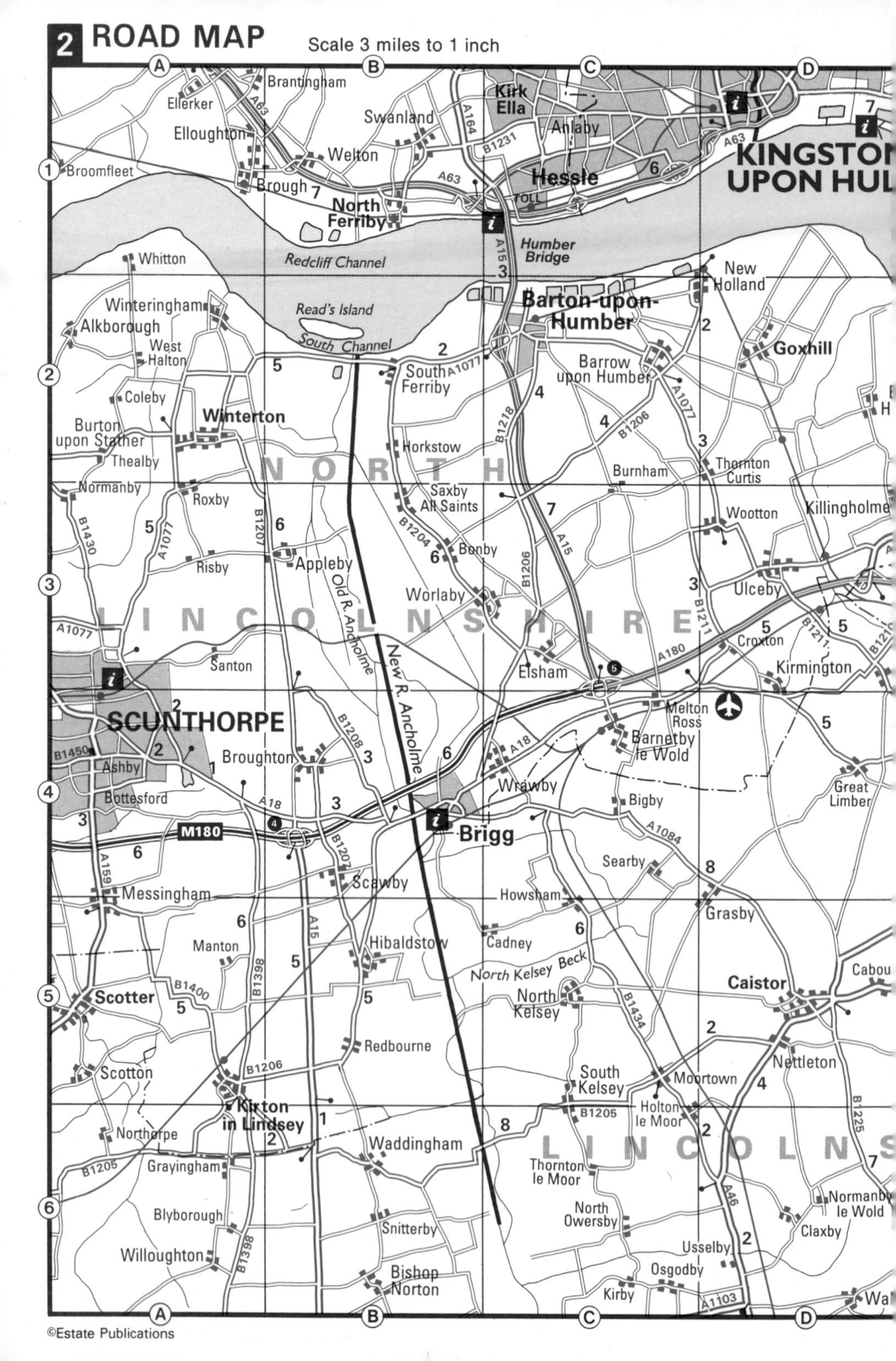

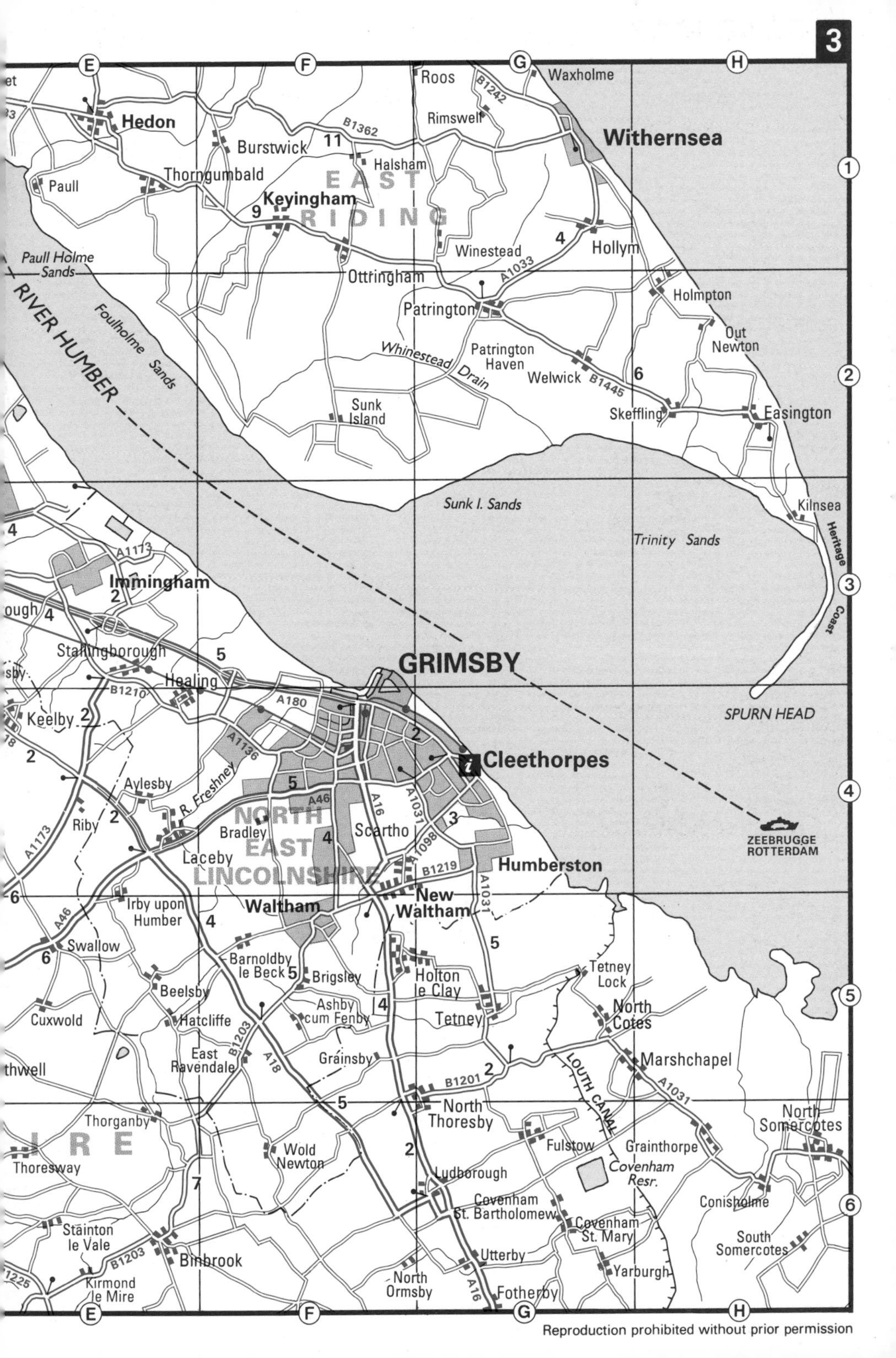
E
F
G
H
Roos
Waxholme
B1242
Rimswell
Hedon
Withernsea
B1362
Burstwick
11
Halsham
Thorngumbald
Paull
EAST
Keyingham
9
RIDING
4
Winestead
Hollym
Paull Holme Sands
Ottringham
A1033
Holmpton
RIVER HUMBER
Foulholme Sands
Patrington
Out Newton
Whinestead Drain
Patrington Haven
Welwick
B1445
6
Skeffling
Easington
Sunk Island
Sunk I. Sands
Kilnsea
Trinity Sands
Heritage Coast
A1173
Immingham
2
4
Stallingborough
5
GRIMSBY
Healing
B1210
A180
Keelby
SPURN HEAD
Cleethorpes
A1136
R. Freshney
Aylesby
5
A46
A16
A1031
NORTH EAST LINCOLNSHIRE
Bradley
Scartho
3
Riby
A1173
4
A1098
Laceby
ZEEBRUGGE ROTTERDAM
Humberston
B1219
New Waltham
Waltham
Irby upon Humber
A1031
A46
Swallow
Barnoldby le Beck
Brigsley
Holton le Clay
Tetney Lock
Beelsby
Cuxwold
Hatcliffe
Ashby cum Fenby
Tetney
North Cotes
East Ravendale
B1203
A18
Grainsby
Marshchapel
LOUTH CANAL
B1201
A1031
Thorganby
North Thoresby
North Somercotes
Fulstow
Grainthorpe
IRE
Thoresway
Wold Newton
Covenham Resr.
Ludborough
7
Covenham St. Bartholomew
Conisholme
Stainton le Vale
Covenham St. Mary
South Somercotes
B1203
Binbrook
Utterby
Yarburgh
Kirmond le Mire
North Ormsby
A16
Fotherby
1
2
3
4
5
6

GRIMSBY CENTRE

Scale 7 inches to 1 mile

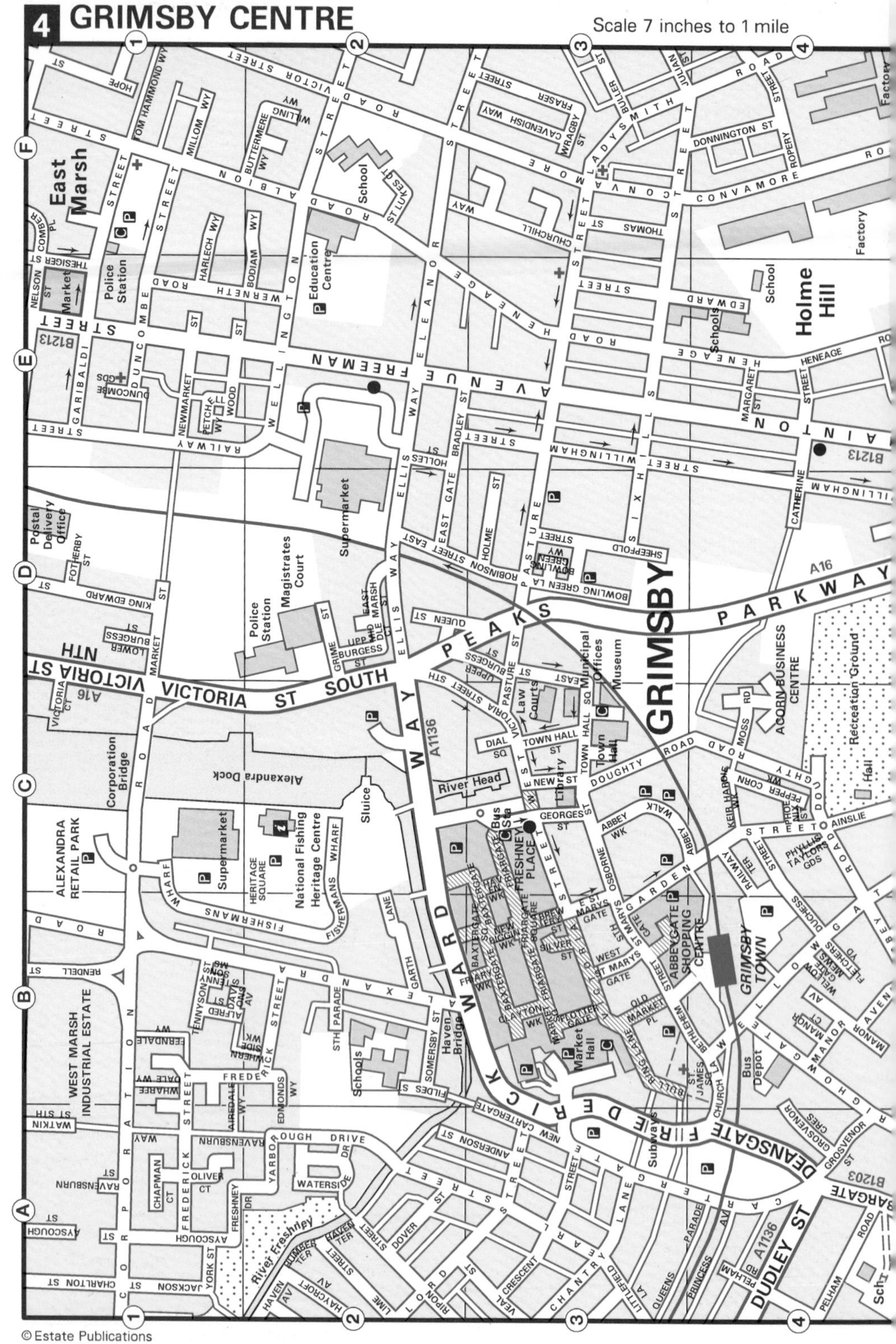

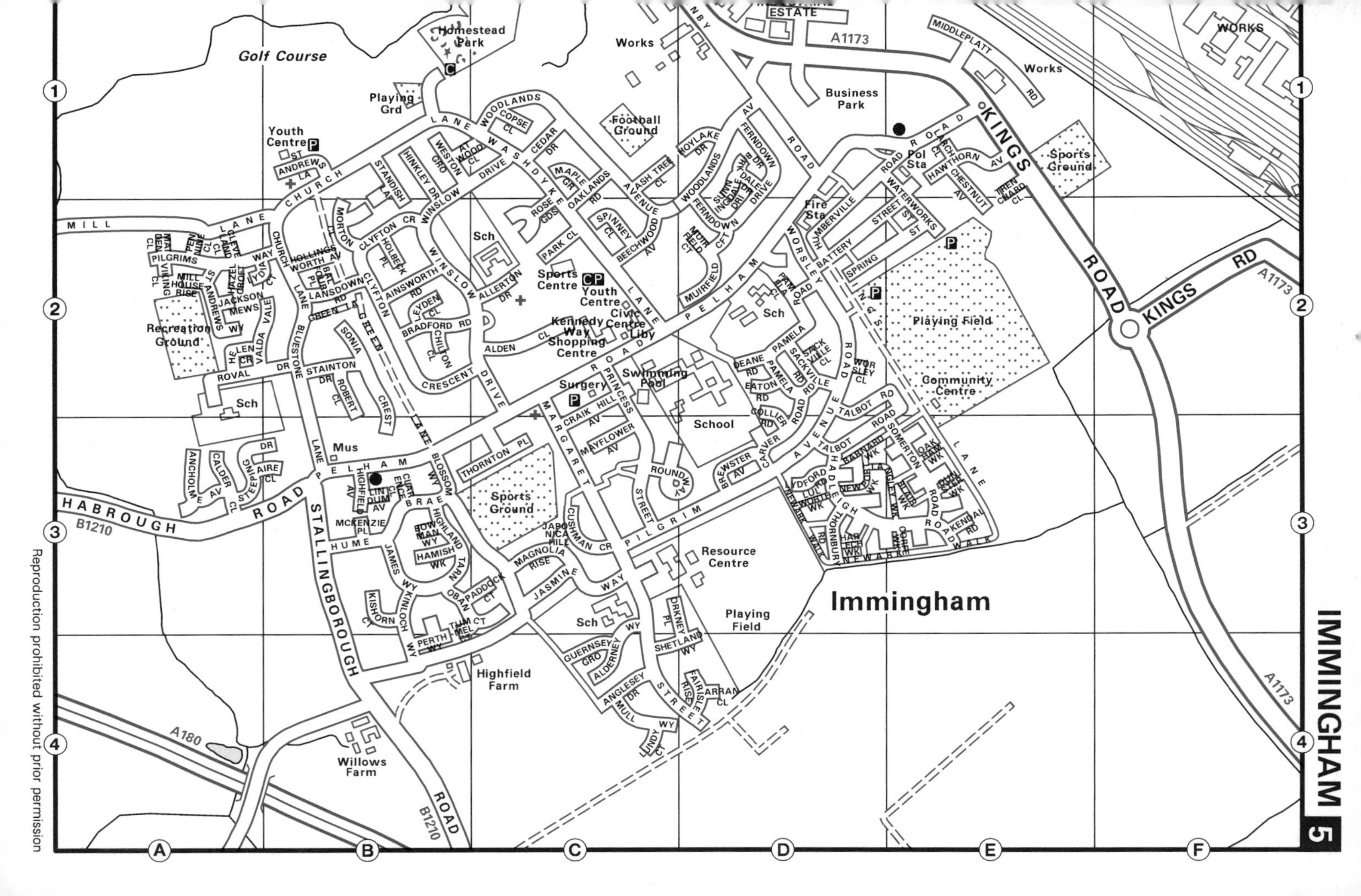

Golf Course
Homestead Park
Works
ESTATE
A1173
MIDDLEPLATT RD
Works
WORKS
Business Park
Playing Grd
Youth Centre
Football Ground
KINGS ROAD
KINGS RD
Sports Ground
Pol Sta
Fire Sta
WATERWORKS ST
HUMBERVILLE
BATTERY ST
SPRING
WORSLEY ROAD
Playing Field
Community Centre
PELHAM ROAD
Sch
School
Swimming Pool
Surgery
Sports Centre
Youth Centre
Civic Centre
Liby
Kennedy Way Shopping Centre
WASHDYKE LANE
WOODLANDS
COPSE CL
CEDAR DR
MAPLE GR
OAKLANDS RD
AVENUE
ASH TREE CL
SPINNEY CL
BEECHWOOD AV
HOYLAKE DR
FERNDOWN DR
WOODLANDS
MUIRFIELD
WESTON GRO
HINKLEY DR
STANDISH LA
WINSLOW DRIVE
CHURCH LANE
MILL LANE
PILGRIMS
VIKING CL
MILL HOUSE RISE
ST ANDREWS
JACKSON MEWS
VALDA VALE
Recreation Ground
ROYAL
BLUESTONE
STAINTON DR
ROBERT CL
SONIA
CREST
GREEN LANE
CLYFTON CR
HOLBECK PL
AINSWORTH RD
LEYDEN CL
BRADFORD RD
CHILTON CL
CRESCENT
ALDEN CL
ALLERTON DR
MORTON CL
HOLLINGSWORTH AV
LANSDOWN
Sch
Mus
ANCHOLME AV
CALDER CL
STEEPING
AIRE CL
HABROUGH ROAD
B1210
STALLINGBOROUGH
HIGHFIELD AV
MCKENZIE PL
HUME
BRAE
BLOSSOM WY
THORNTON PL
Sports Ground
HIGHLAND TARN
HAMISH WK
JAMES WY
KINLOCH WY
KISHORN CT
OBAN
PADDOCK CT
PERTH WY
Highfield Farm
Willows Farm
A180
ROAD
MARGARET STREET
CRAIK HILL AV
MAYFLOWER AV
PRINCESS
ROUNDWAY
MAGNOLIA RISE
CUSHMAN CR
JASMINE WAY
GUERNSEY GRO
ALDERNEY
ANGLESEY DR
MULL WY
LUNDY CT
ORKNEY PL
SHETLAND WY
FAIRISLE RISE
ARRAN CL
STREET
PILGRIM
Resource Centre
Playing Field
Immingham
BREWSTER AV
CARVER
COLLIER RD
PAMELA RD
SACKVILLE RD
DEANE RD
EATON RD
WORSLEY CL
TALBOT AVENUE
TALBOT RD
SOMERTON ROAD
HADLEIGH
THORNBURY
NEWARK WALK
KENDAL RD
LANE
A1173
1
2
3
4
A
B
C
D
E
F

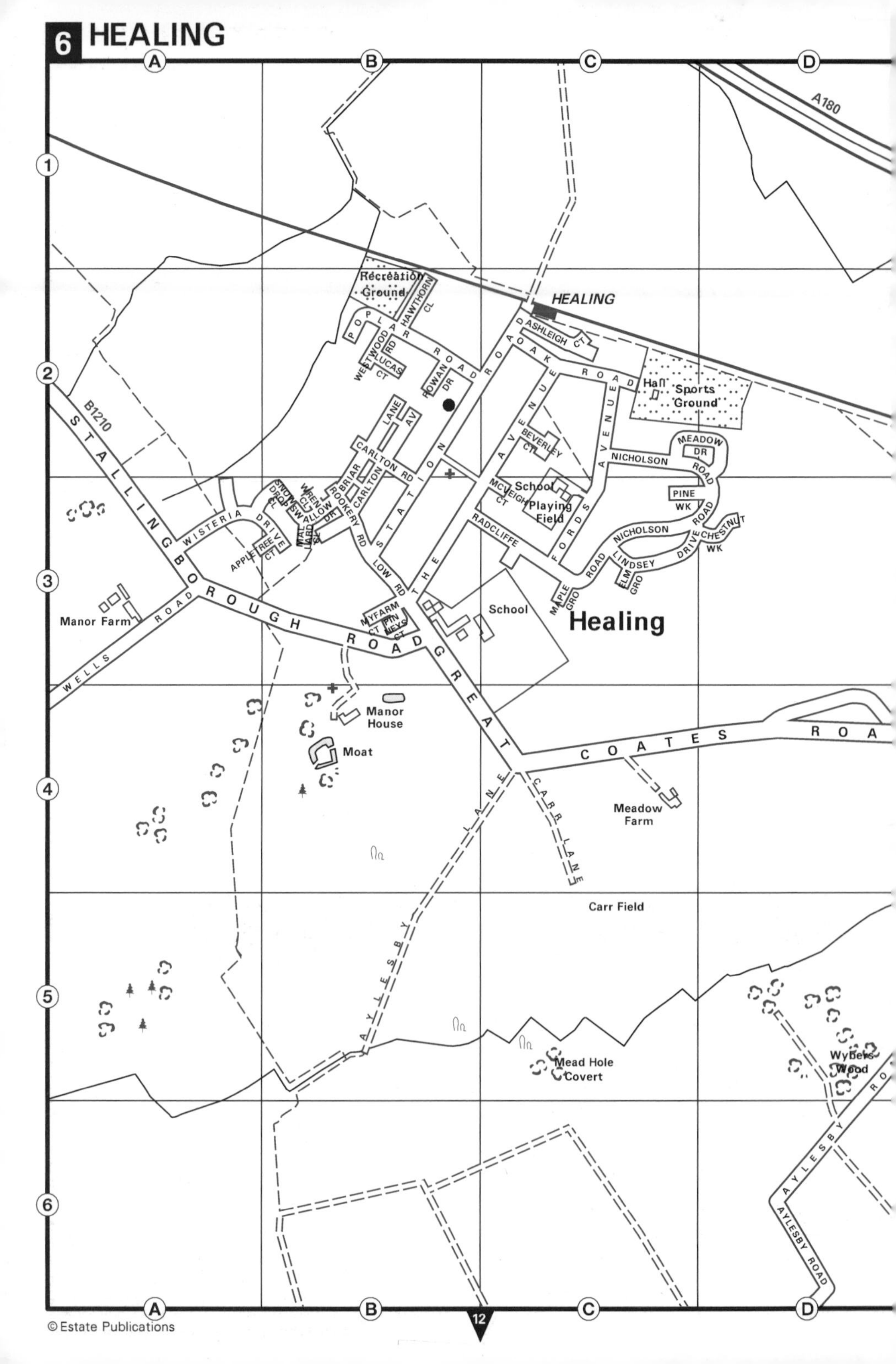
HEALING
A180
B1210
STALLINGBOROUGH ROAD
WELLS ROAD
Manor Farm
WISTERIA DRIVE
APPLETREE CT
Recreation Ground
HAWTHORN CL
POPLAR ROAD
WESTWOOD RD
LUCAS CT
ROWAN DR
LANE AV
CARLTON RD
BRIAR
CARLTON
ROOKERY RD
WREN CL
SWALLOW DR
SNOWDROP CL
MALLARD CL
STATION ROAD
THE
LOW RD
MYFARM CT
PINNEYS CT
ASHLEIGH CT
OAK ROAD
AVENUE
BEVERLEY CT
MCVEIGH CT
School
Playing Field
RADCLIFFE
FORDS AVENUE
Hall
Sports Ground
MEADOW DR
MEADOW ROAD
NICHOLSON
PINE WK
NICHOLSON ROAD
CHESTNUT WK
DRIVE
LINDSEY
ELM GRO
MAPLE GRO
School
Healing
Manor House
Moat
GREAT COATES ROAD
CARR LANE
Meadow Farm
AYLESBY LANE
Carr Field
Mead Hole Covert
Wybers Wood
AYLESBY ROAD

12

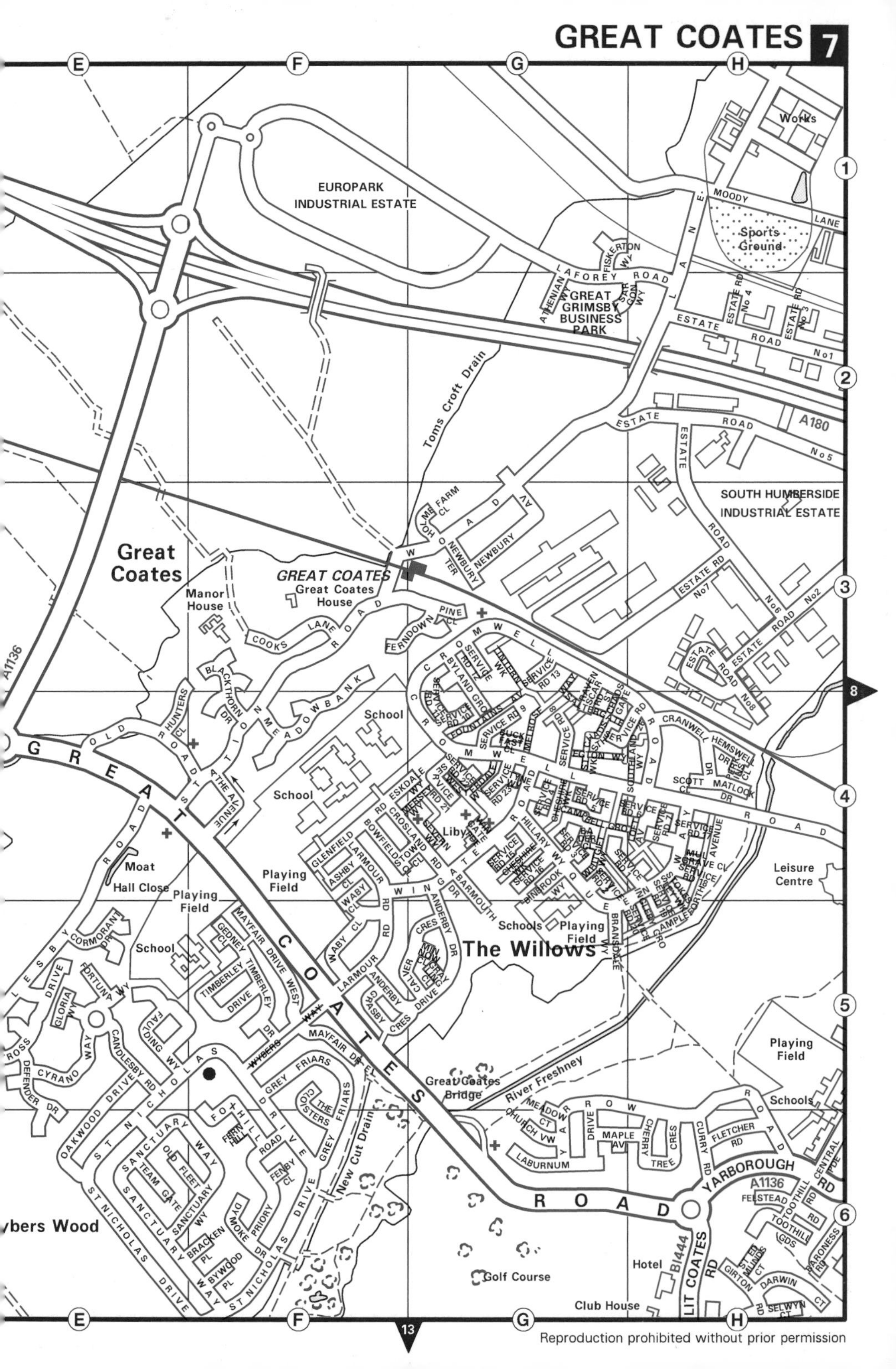
EUROPARK
INDUSTRIAL ESTATE
GREAT
GRIMSBY
BUSINESS
PARK
SOUTH HUMBERSIDE
INDUSTRIAL ESTATE
Great
Coates
GREAT COATES
Great Coates
House
Manor
House
Toms Croft Drain
School
Playing
Field
Moat
Hall Close
The Willows
Leisure
Centre
Great Coates
Bridge
River Freshney
New Cut Drain
Golf Course
Hotel
Club House
Playing
Field
Schools
Sports
Ground
Works
A180
A1136
B1444
Wybers Wood
YARBOROUGH RD
GREAT COATES ROAD

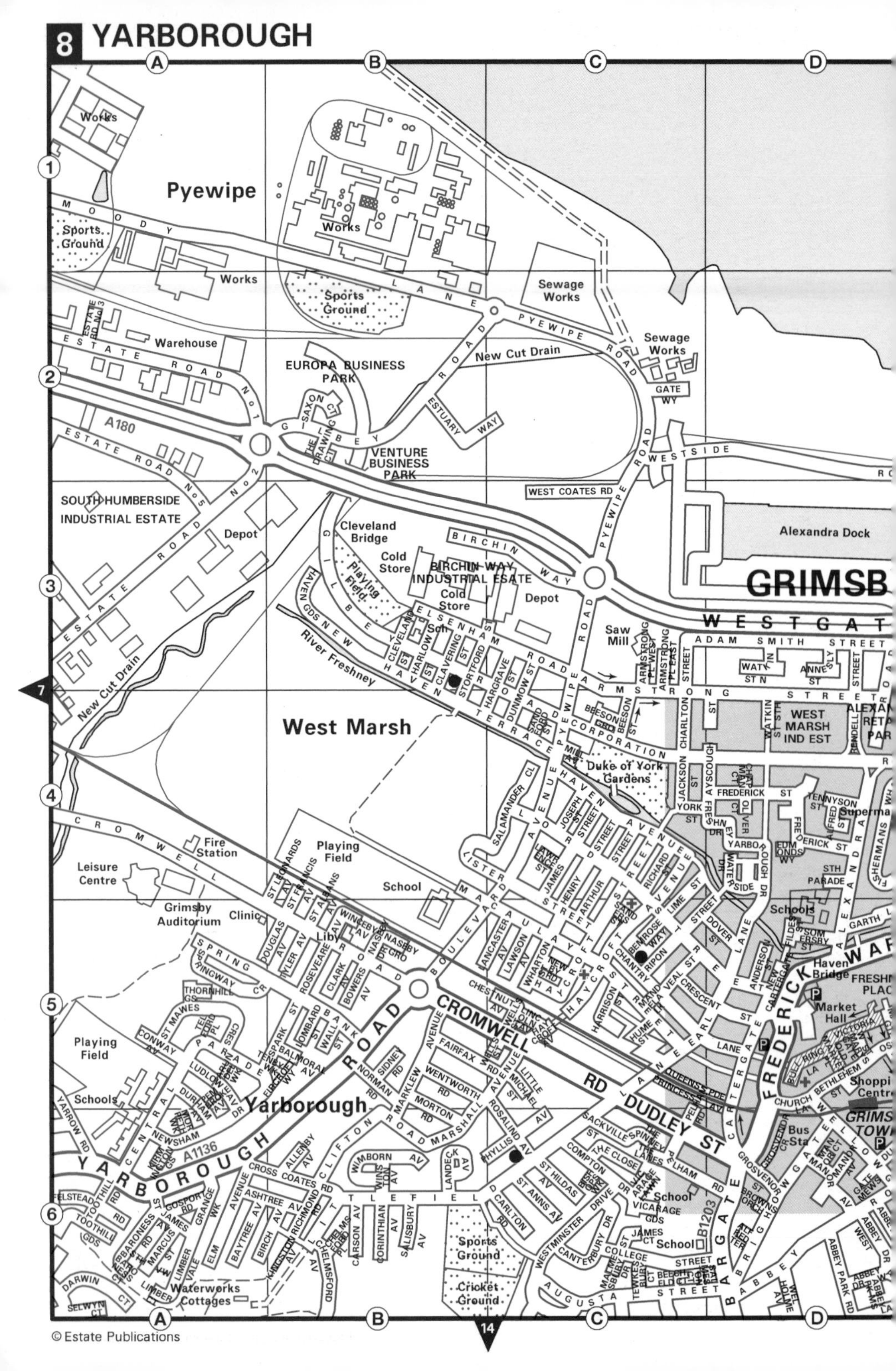
Pyewipe
Works
Sports Ground
Works
Sewage Works
Sewage Works
EUROPA BUSINESS PARK
VENTURE BUSINESS PARK
Warehouse
SOUTH HUMBERSIDE INDUSTRIAL ESTATE
Depot
Cleveland Bridge
Cold Store
BIRCHIN WAY INDUSTRIAL ESATE
Depot
Playing Field
Saw Mill
Alexandra Dock
GRIMSB
WEST MARSH IND EST
West Marsh
River Freshney
New Cut Drain
Duke of York Gardens
Fire Station
Leisure Centre
Grimsby Auditorium
Clinic
Playing Field
School
Liby
Playing Field
Schools
Yarborough
Waterworks Cottages
Sports Ground
Cricket Ground
School
School
Schools
Haven Bridge
Market Hall
Bus Sta
Shopping Centre
MOODY LANE
PYEWIPE ROAD
ESTATE ROAD No 1
ESTATE ROAD No 2
ESTATE ROAD No 5
ESTATE ROAD No 3
ESTUARY WAY
GILBEY ROAD
WEST COATES RD
WESTSIDE
WESTGATE
ARMSTRONG STREET
ADAM SMITH STREET
CORPORATION
BIRCHIN WAY
HAVEN AVENUE
CROMWELL ROAD
CROMWELL RD
DUDLEY ST
YARBOROUGH ROAD
LITTLEFIELD
FREDERICK WARD
CARTERGATE
BARGATE
AUGUSTA STREET
A180
A1136
B1203

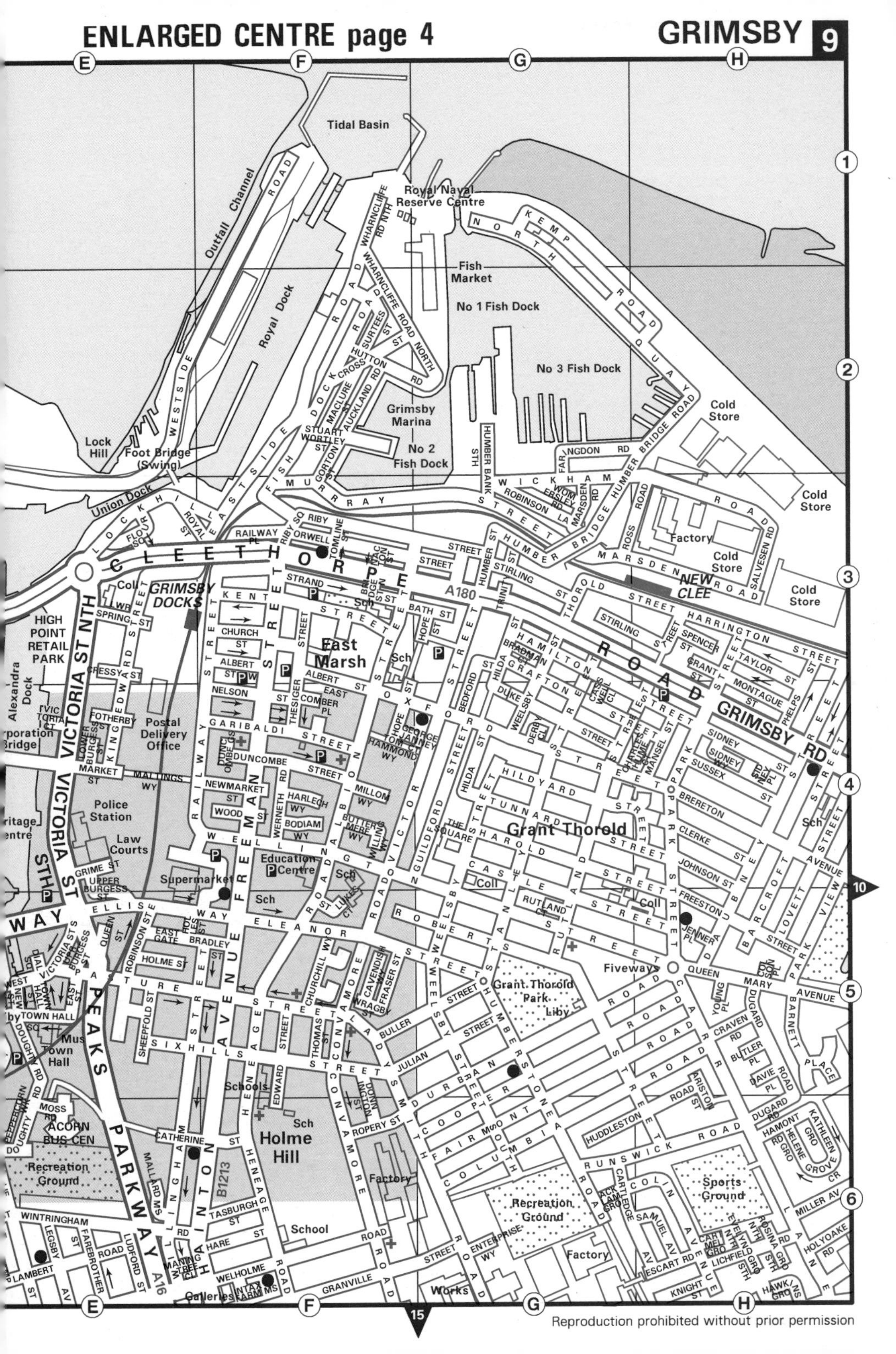
Tidal Basin
Royal Naval Reserve Centre
Outfall Channel
Royal Dock
Fish Market
No 1 Fish Dock
No 3 Fish Dock
Grimsby Marina
No 2 Fish Dock
Lock Hill
Foot Bridge (Swing)
Union Dock
Cold Store
Factory
NEW CLEE
GRIMSBY DOCKS
HIGH POINT RETAIL PARK
Alexandra Dock
Postal Delivery Office
Police Station
Law Courts
Supermarket
Education Centre
East Marsh
Grant Thorold
Grant Thorold Park
Liby
Fiveways
Holme Hill
Schools
School
Town Hall
Mus
ACORN BUS CEN
Recreation Ground
Sports Ground
Works
Galleries
VICTORIA ST NTH
VICTORIA ST
PEAKS PARKWAY
CLEETHORPE ROAD
GRIMSBY RD
FREEMAN AVENUE
VICTOR STREET
WELLINGTON STREET
ELEANOR STREET
HAINTON AVENUE
HUMBER BRIDGE ROAD
KEMP ROAD
NORTH QUAY
FISH DOCK ROAD
WHARNCLIFFE ROAD NORTH
WESTSIDE ROAD
EASTSIDE ROAD
MURRAY STREET
WICKHAM STREET
MARSDEN ROAD
HUMBER STREET
STIRLING STREET
THOROLD STREET
HARRINGTON STREET
HILDYARD STREET
TUNNARD STREET
HAROLD STREET
CASTLE STREET
RUTLAND STREET
ROBERTS STREET
PARK STREET
QUEEN MARY AVENUE
SIXHILLS STREET
CONVAMORE ROAD
DURBAN ROAD
COOPER ROAD
FAIRMONT ROAD
COLUMBIA ROAD
RUNSWICK ROAD
HUDDLESTON ROAD
GRANVILLE STREET
WELHOLME ROAD
WINTRINGHAM ROAD
LAMBERT ROAD
A180
A16
B1213
E
F
G
H
1
2
3
4
5
6
10
15

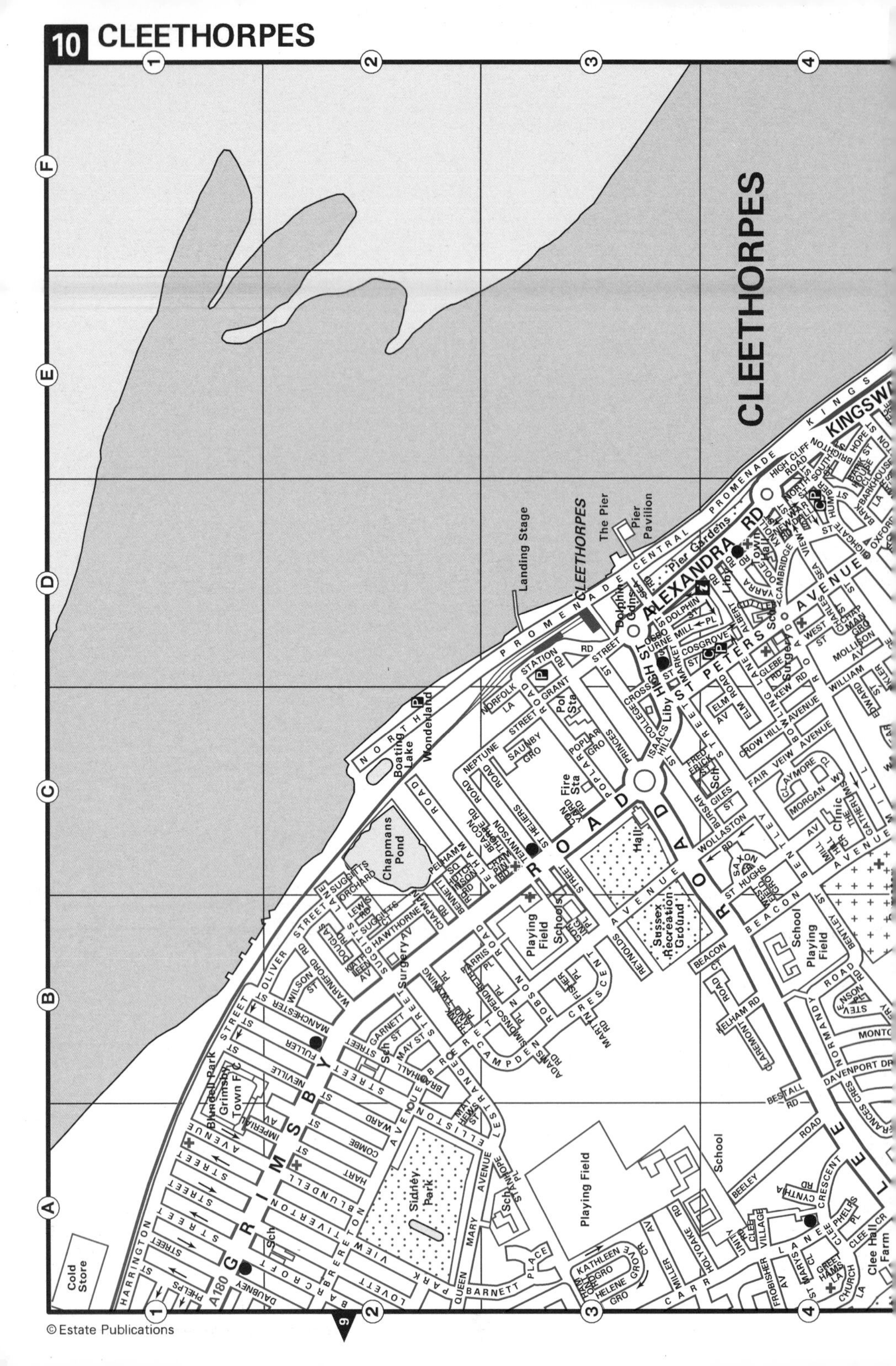
CLEETHORPES
KINGSWAY
CENTRAL PROMENADE
NORTH PROMENADE
ALEXANDRA RD
HIGH ST
ST PETERS AVENUE
GRIMSBY ROAD
The Pier
Pier Pavilion
Pier Gardens
Landing Stage
Boating Lake
Wonderland
Chapmans Pond
Sussex Recreation Ground
Sidney Park
Playing Field
Blundell Park
Grimsby Town F.C.
Cold Store
Fire Sta
Pol Sta
Clinic
Schools
Clee Hall Farm

Cleethorpes Golf Course
Cleethorpes Country Park
Boating Lake
Miniature Railway
Marine Walk
Leisure Centre
Cricket Ground
Schools
Haverstoe Park
King George V Playing Field
Playing Field
School
Superstore
BUSINESS PARK
INDUSTRIAL ESTATE
Hewitts Circus
Peaks Covert
Peaks Covert Farm
HUMBERSTON ROAD
GRIMSBY ROAD
TAYLORS AVENUE
HEWITTS AVENUE
QUEENS PARADE
Buck Beck
A1031
A1098

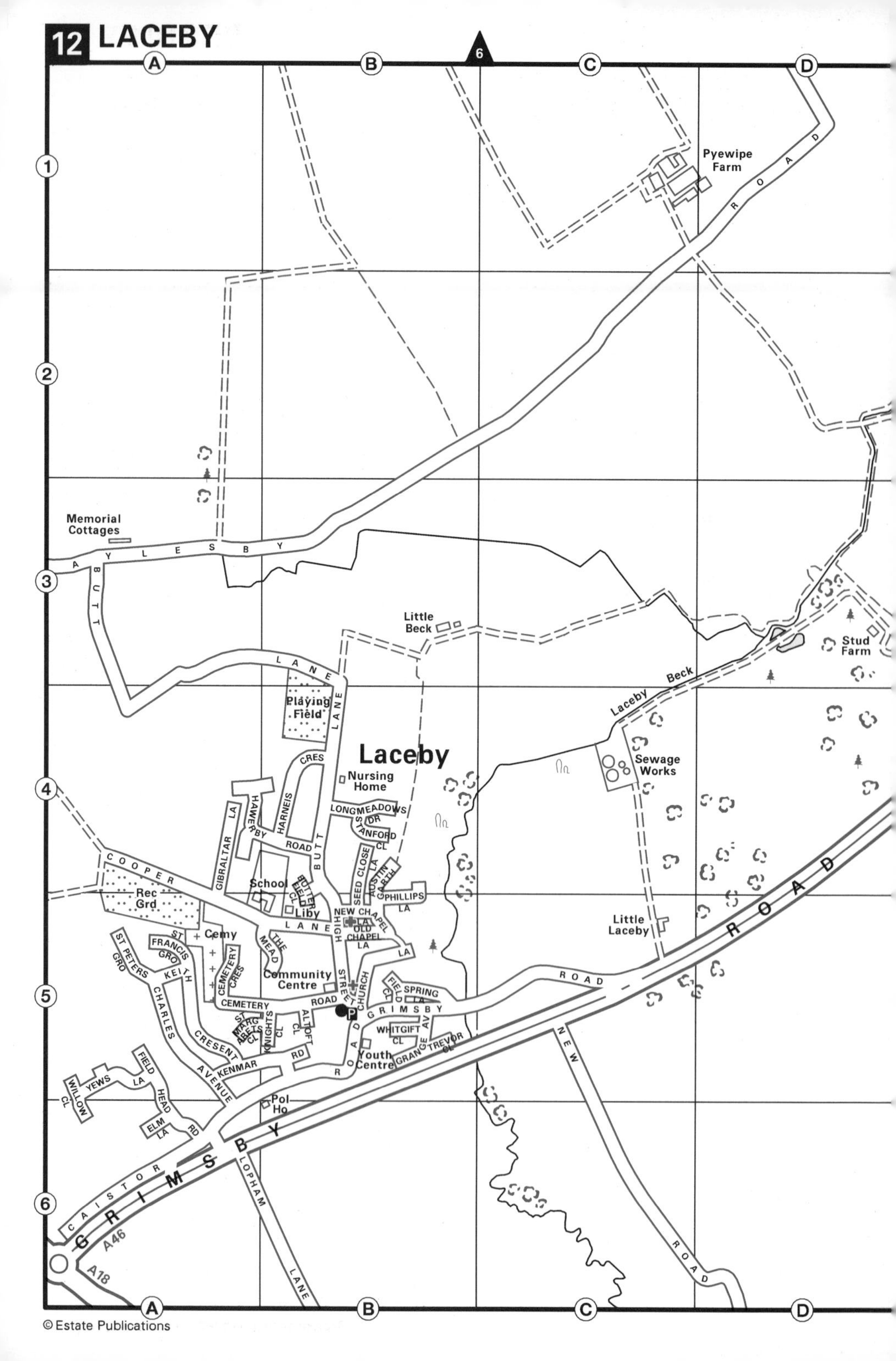
Pyewipe Farm
ROAD
Memorial Cottages
AYLESBY
BUTT
LANE
Little Beck
Stud Farm
Laceby Beck
Playing Field
Laceby
Sewage Works
CRES
Nursing Home
HAWERBY
HARNEIS
LONGMEADOWS DR
STANFORD CL
ROAD
BUTT
GIBRALTAR LA
COOPER
SEED CLOSE
AUSTIN GARTH
PHILLIPS LA
School
BUTTER FIELD CL
Rec Grd
Liby
NEW CHAPEL LA
OLD CHAPEL LA
HIGH
LANE
Little Laceby
ST FRANCIS GRO
Cemy
THE MEAD
ST PETERS GRO
KEITH
CEMETERY CRES
Community Centre
STREET
CHURCH
FIELD CL
SPRING LA
ROAD
CHARLES
CEMETERY
ROAD
GRIMSBY
ST MARGARETS CL
KNIGHTS CL
ALTOFT CL
WHITGIFT CL
GRANGE AV
TREVOR CL
CRESENT
RD
Youth Centre
NEW
WILLOW CL
YEWS LA
FIELD HEAD RD
AVENUE
KENMAR
Pol Ho
ELM LA
GRIMSBY
CAISTOR
LOPHAM
LANE
A46
A18
ROAD

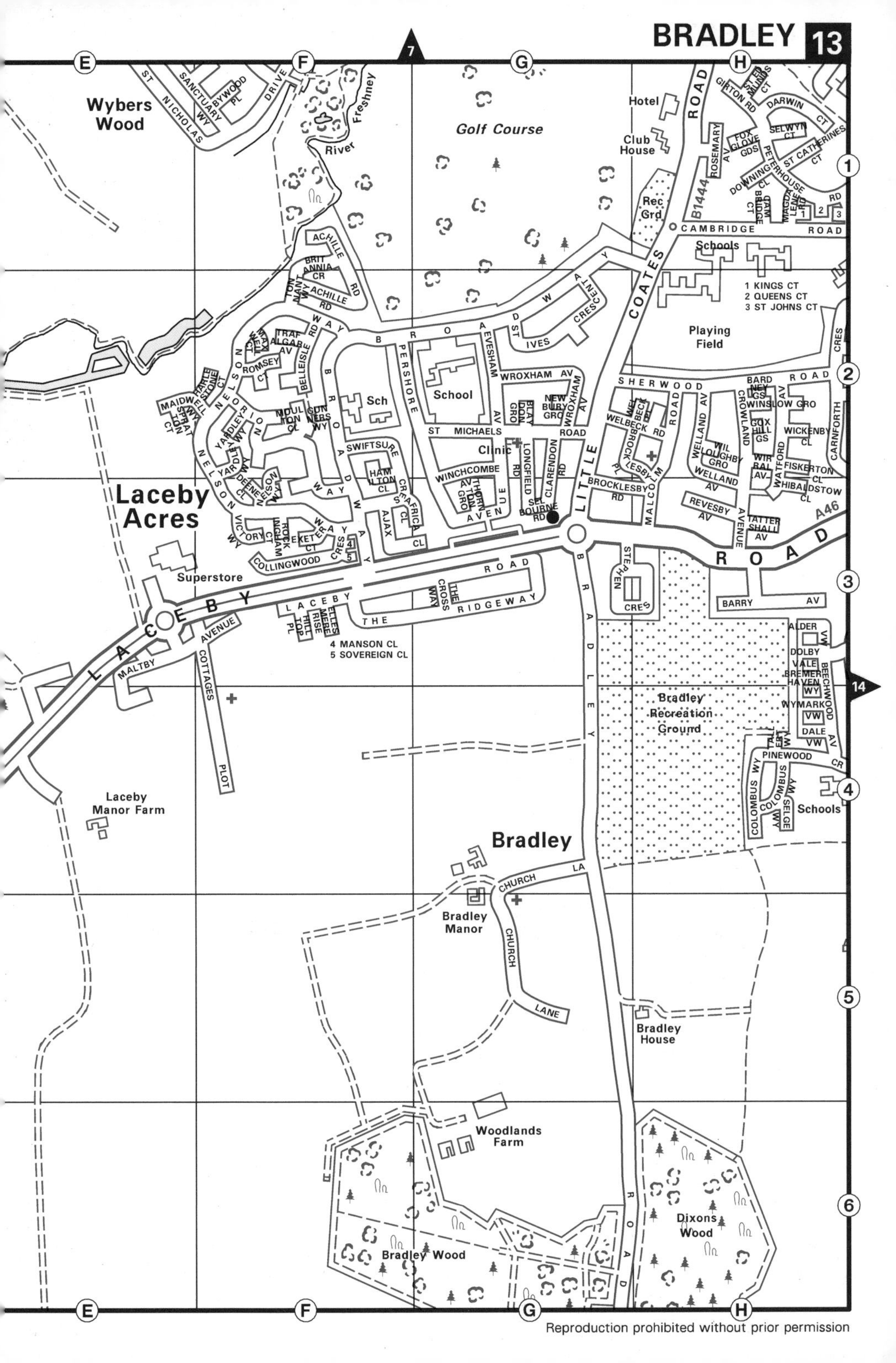
Wybers Wood
Golf Course
River Freshney
Hotel
Club House
Rec Grd
Schools
1 KINGS CT
2 QUEENS CT
3 ST JOHNS CT
Playing Field
Laceby Acres
Superstore
4 MANSON CL
5 SOVEREIGN CL
School
Sch
Clinic
Bradley Recreation Ground
Schools
Laceby Manor Farm
Bradley
Bradley Manor
Bradley House
Woodlands Farm
Bradley Wood
Dixons Wood
LACEBY ROAD
LITTLE COATES ROAD
CAMBRIDGE ROAD
SHERWOOD ROAD
BRADLEY ROAD
BROADWAY
ST MICHAELS ROAD
CHURCH LANE
A46
B1444

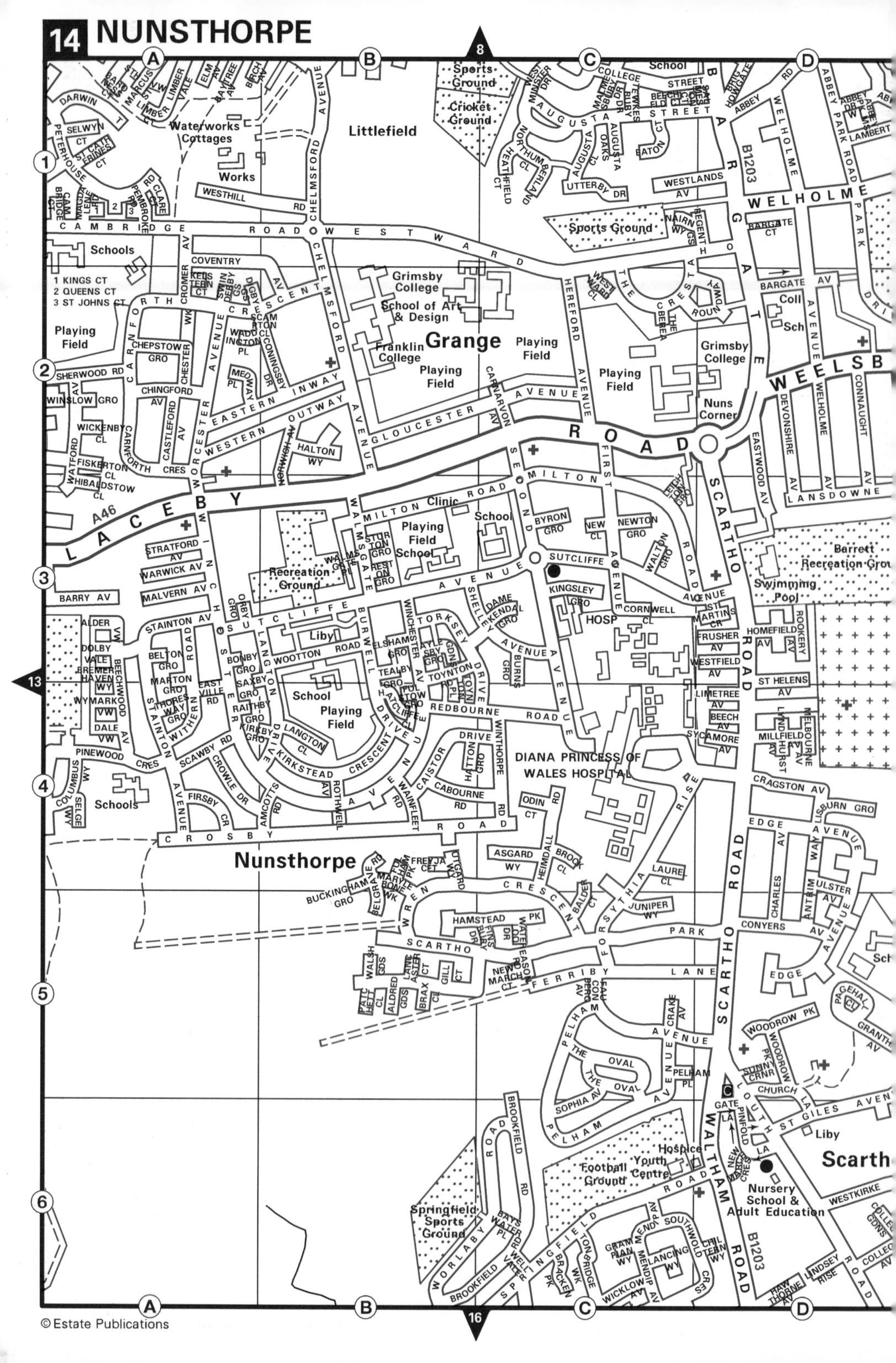
14
NUNSTHORPE
Waterworks Cottages
Works
Littlefield
Sports Ground
Cricket Ground
School
Schools
1 KINGS CT
2 QUEENS CT
3 ST JOHNS CT
Playing Field
Grimsby College
School of Art & Design
Franklin College
Grange
Playing Field
Grimsby College
Nuns Corner
CAMBRIDGE ROAD
WESTWARD
WESTHILL RD
CHELMSFORD AVENUE
WELHOLME
BARGATE
WEELSBY ROAD
LACEBY ROAD
A46
B1203
SCARTHO ROAD
MILTON ROAD
Clinic
SUTCLIFFE AVENUE
Recreation Ground
Liby
HOSP
Barrett Recreation Ground
Swimming Pool
School
Playing Field
DIANA PRINCESS OF WALES HOSPITAL
Nunsthorpe
CROSBY ROAD
SCARTHO PARK
FERRIBY LANE
PELHAM AVENUE
THE OVAL
WALTHAM ROAD
Football Ground
Youth Centre
Hospice
Springfield Sports Ground
Nursery School & Adult Education
Scarth
Liby
ST GILES AVENUE
CHURCH LA
Schools
A
B
C
D
1
2
3
4
5
6
8
13
16

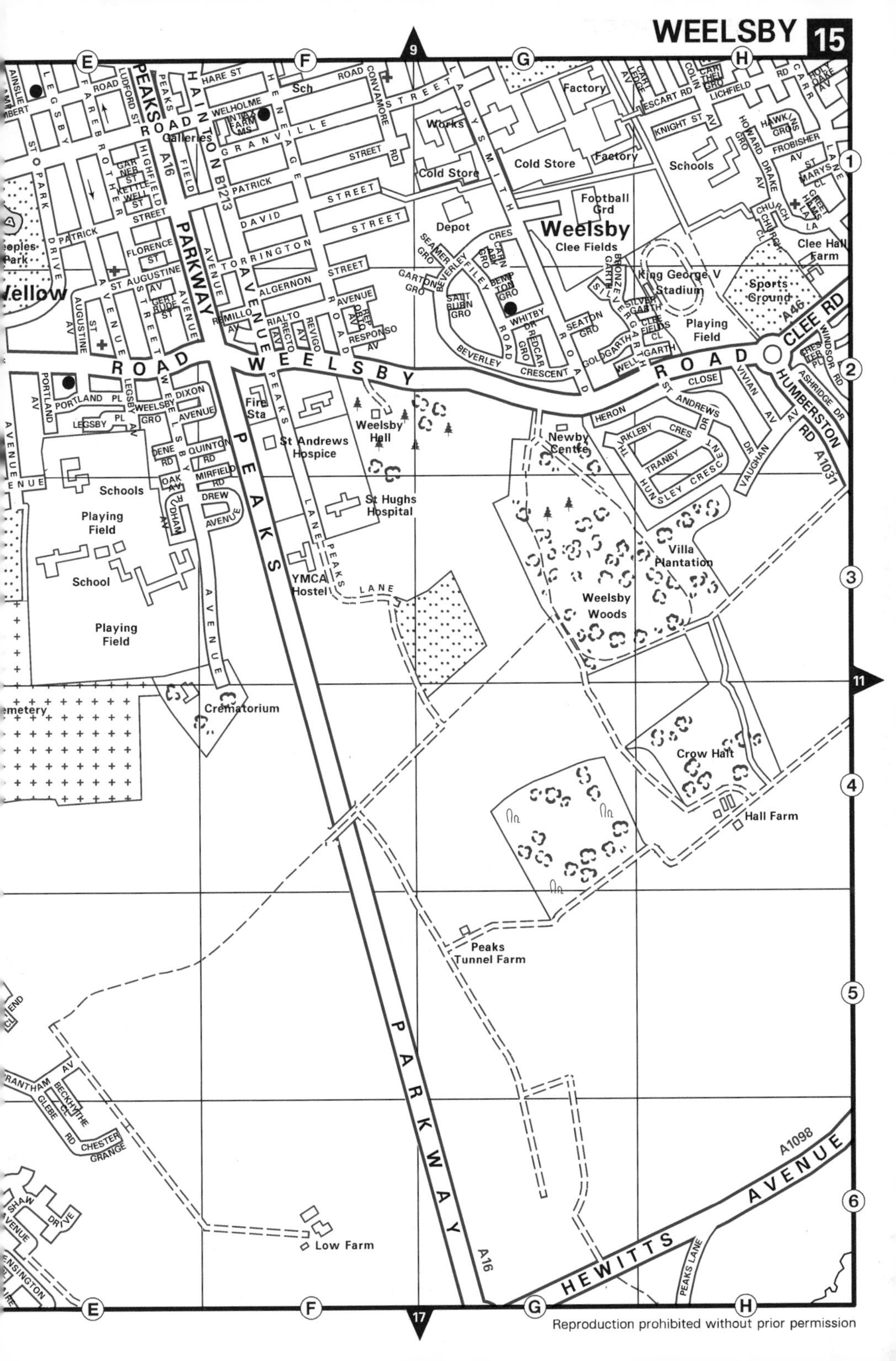
Weelsby
Clee Fields
Peoples Park
Weelsby Hall
St Andrews Hospice
St Hughs Hospital
YMCA Hostel
Fire Sta
Crematorium
Cemetery
Schools
Playing Field
School
Factory
Cold Store
Works
Depot
Football Grd
King George V Stadium
Sports Ground
Clee Hall Farm
Newby Centre
Villa Plantation
Weelsby Woods
Crow Halt
Hall Farm
Peaks Tunnel Farm
Low Farm
Galleries
PEAKS PARKWAY
WEELSBY ROAD
HEWITTS AVENUE
CLEE RD
HUMBERSTON RD
A16
A46
A1031
A1098
B1213

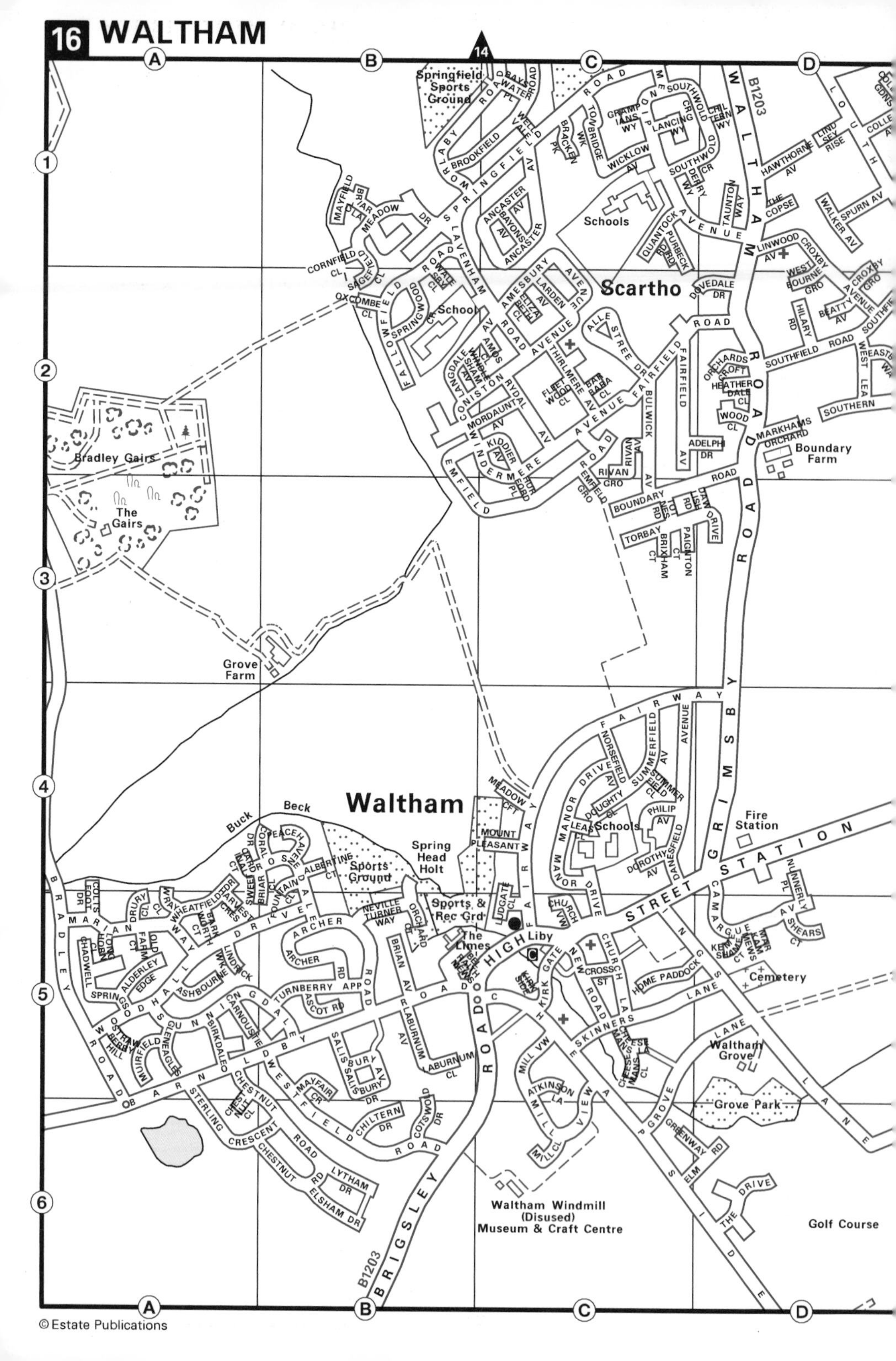

Springfield Sports Ground
Schools
Scartho
School
Bradley Gairs
The Gairs
Grove Farm
Boundary Farm
Waltham
Buck Beck
Spring Head Holt
Sports Ground
Sports & Rec Grd
The Limes
Liby
Fire Station
Cemetery
Waltham Grove
Grove Park
Waltham Windmill (Disused) Museum & Craft Centre
Golf Course
B1203

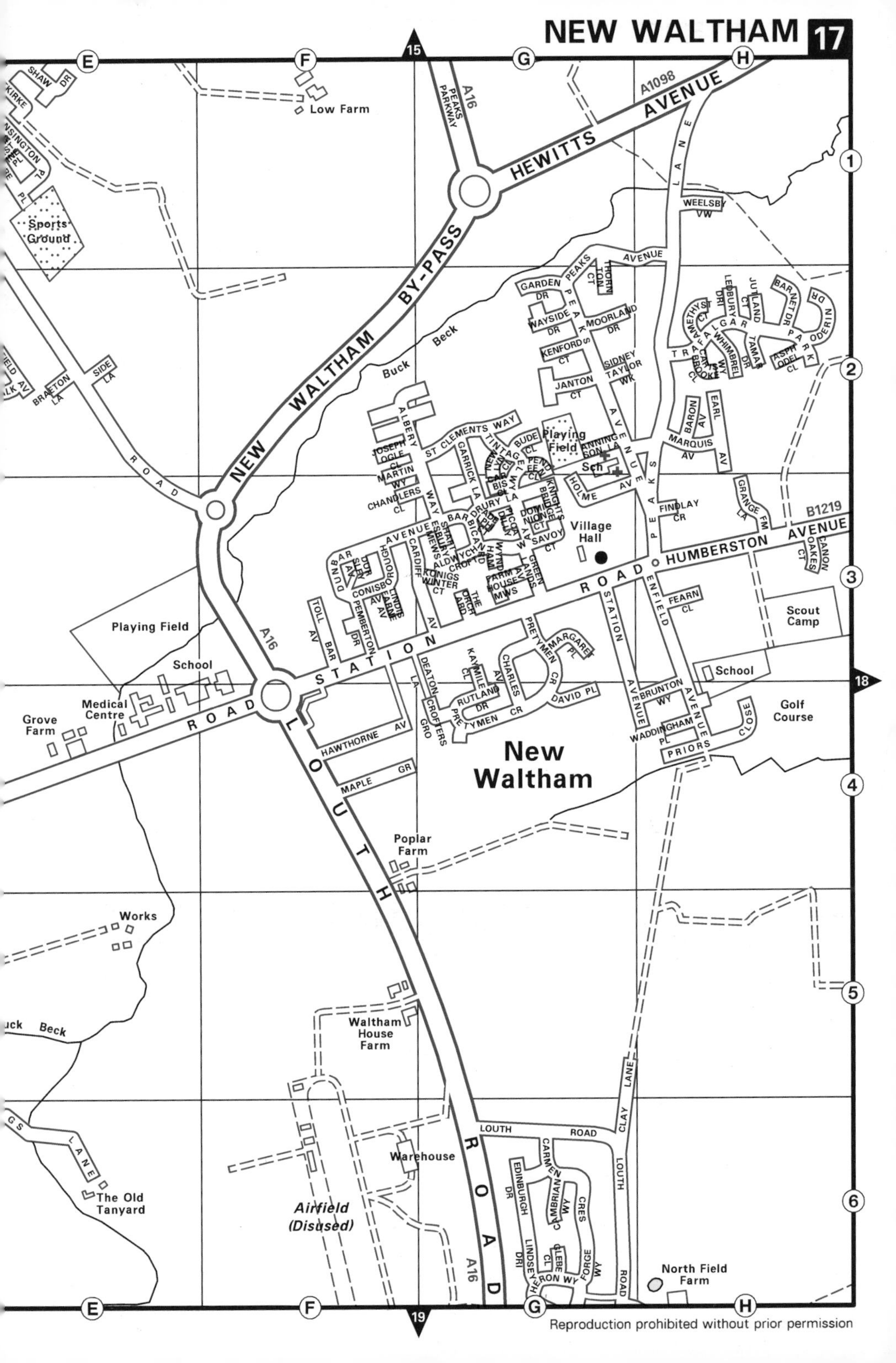
New Waltham
NEW WALTHAM BY-PASS
HEWITTS AVENUE
A1098
A16
PEAKS PARKWAY
Low Farm
Sports Ground
Buck Beck
Playing Field
School
Medical Centre
Grove Farm
STATION ROAD
HUMBERSTON AVENUE
B1219
LOUTH ROAD
Village Hall
Scout Camp
Golf Course
Poplar Farm
Works
Waltham House Farm
Warehouse
Airfield (Disused)
The Old Tanyard
North Field Farm
CLAY LANE
PEAKS LANE
PEAKS AVENUE
STATION AVENUE
ENFIELD AVENUE
HAWTHORNE AV
MAPLE GR
CROFTERS
DEATON
PRETYMEN CR
RUTLAND DR
CHARLES AV
MARGARET PL
DAVID PL
BRUNTON WY
WADDINGHAM PL
PRIORS CLOSE
FEARN CL
CANON OAKES CT
GRANGE FM LA
FINDLAY CR
TRAFALGAR PARK
MARQUIS AV
BARON AV
EARL AV
WEELSBY VW
ST CLEMENTS WAY
CHANDLERS WAY
TOLL BAR AV
CONISBOROUGH AV
PEMBERTON DR
DUNBAR AV
KONIGS WINTER CT
CARDIFF AV
THE ORCHARD
FARM HOUSE MWS
GARDEN DR
WAYSIDE DR
KENFORD CT
JANTON CT
MOORLAND DR
SIDNEY TAYLOR WK
HOLME AV
SAVOY CT
EDINBURGH DR
CARMEN CRES
CAMBRIAN WY
LINDSEY DRI
HERON WY
GLEBE CL
FORGE WY
BRAETON LA
SIDE LA
SHAW DR
15
18
19
E
F
G
H
1
2
3
4
5
6

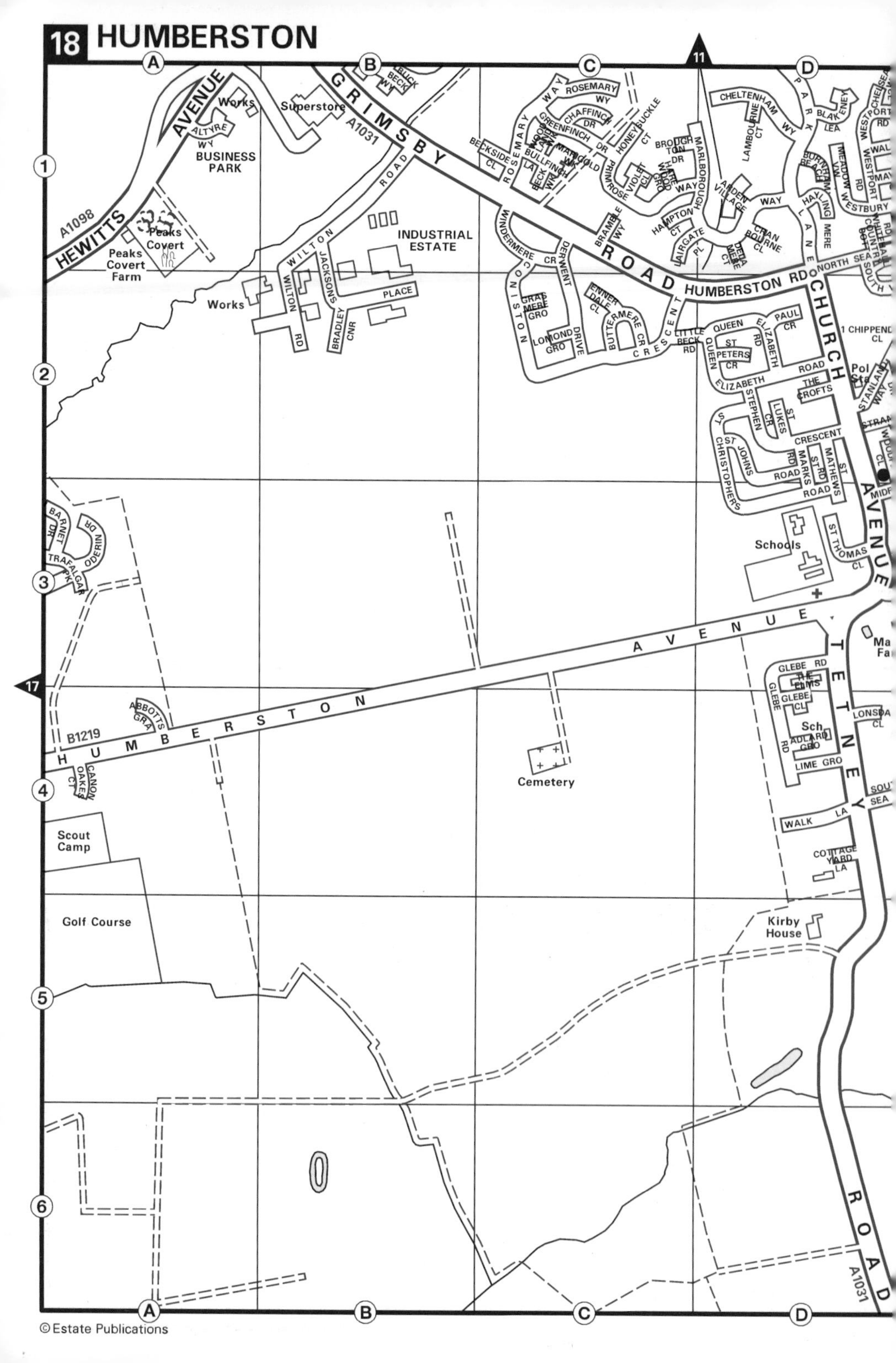
HEWITTS AVENUE
A1098
Works
ALTYRE WY
BUSINESS PARK
Peaks Covert
Peaks Covert Farm
Superstore
GRIMSBY ROAD
A1031
WILTON ROAD
WILTON RD
JACKSONS PLACE
BRADLEY CNR
INDUSTRIAL ESTATE
Works
BUCK BECK WY
ROSEMARY WY
CHAFFINCH DR
GREENFINCH DR
HONEYSUCKLE CT
MARIGOLD WK
BULLFINCH WK
BECKSIDE CL
PRIMROSE
VIOLET CL
BROUGHTON DR
MARLBOROUGH WAY
ARDEN VILLAGE
HAMPTON CT
LAIRGATE PL
CRANBOURNE CL
CHELTENHAM WY
LAMBOURNE CT
PARK
BLAKENEY LEA
BURNHAM BEACH
MEADOW VW
HAYLING MERE
WESTPORT RD
WESTBURY
BRAMBLE WY
WINDERMERE CR
CONISTON
DERWENT DRIVE
GRASMERE GRO
LOMOND GRO
ENNERDALE CL
BUTTERMERE CR
CRESCENT
HUMBERSTON RD
NORTH SEA
LITTLE BECK RD
QUEEN ELIZABETH RD
ST PETERS CR
PAUL CR
ROAD
THE CROFTS
STEPHEN CR
ST LUKES
CRESCENT
ST CHRISTOPHERS
ST JOHNS RD
ST MARKS ROAD
ST MATHEWS RD
ROAD
CHURCH AVENUE
1 CHIPPENDALE CL
Schools
ST THOMAS CL
BARNET DR
ODERIN DR
TRAFALGAR PK
ABBOTTS GRA
B1219
HUMBERSTON AVENUE
CANON OAKES CT
Cemetery
GLEBE RD
THE ELMS
GLEBE CL
Sch
ADLARD GRO
LIME GRO
LONSDALE CL
WALK LA
COTTAGE YARD LA
TETNEY ROAD
Kirby House
Scout Camp
Golf Course
A1031
17
11

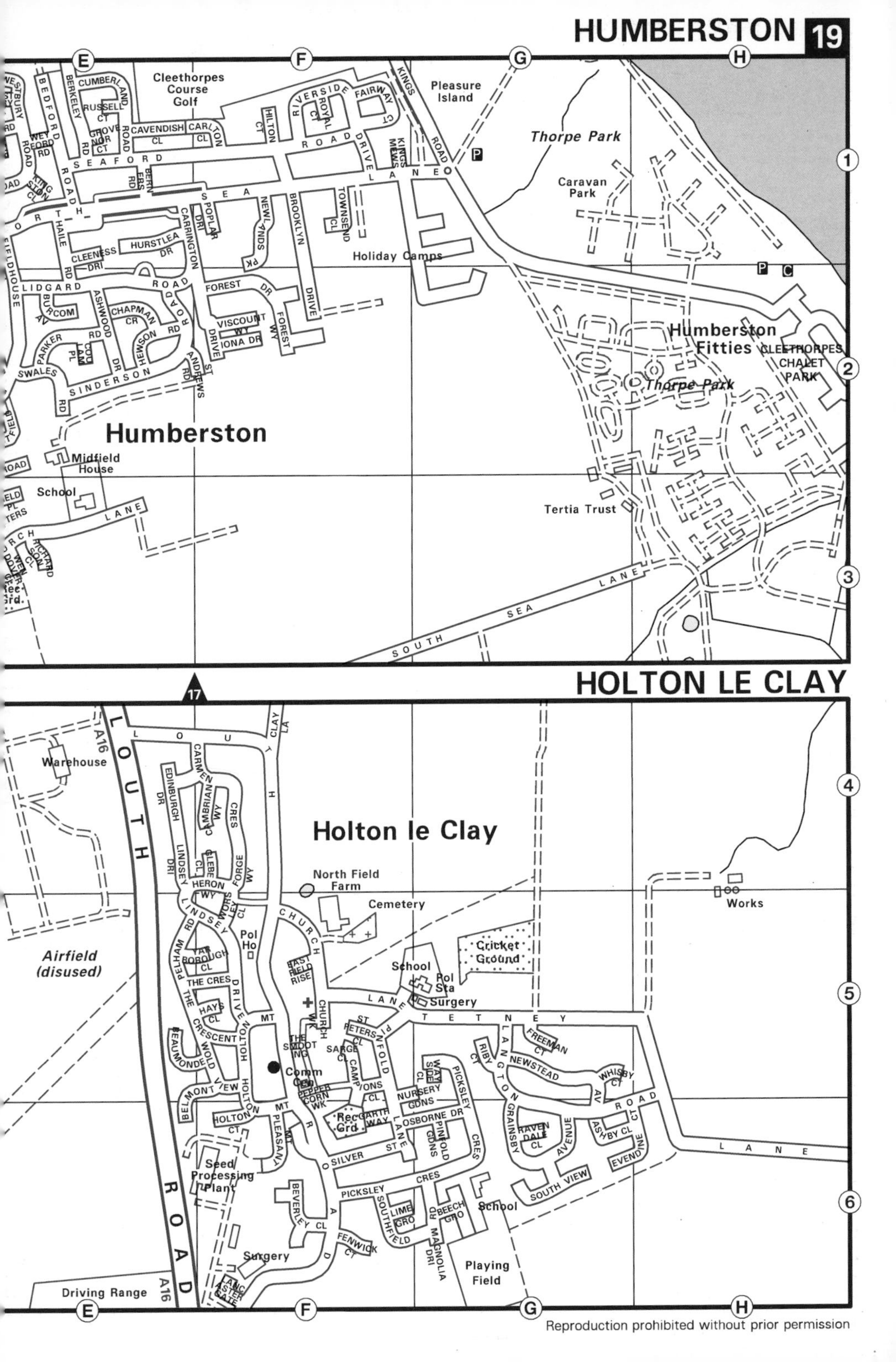
Cleethorpes Course Golf
Pleasure Island
Thorpe Park
Caravan Park
Holiday Camps
Humberston Fitties
CLEETHORPES CHALET PARK
Thorpe Park
Humberston
Midfield House
School
Tertia Trust
SOUTH SEA LANE
HOLTON LE CLAY
17
Holton le Clay
Warehouse
North Field Farm
Cemetery
Works
Airfield (disused)
Cricket Ground
School
Pol Sta
Surgery
Pol Ho
Comm Cen
Rec Grd
Seed Processing Plant
Surgery
School
Playing Field
Driving Range
LOUTH ROAD
TETNEY LANE
A16

A - Z INDEX TO STREETS
with Postcodes

The Index includes some names for which there is insufficient space on the maps. These names are preceded by an * and are followed by the nearest adjoining thoroughfare.

GRIMSBY/ CLEETHORPES

Abbey Dri East. DN32 8 D6
Abbey Dri West. DN32 8 D6
Abbey Pk Mews. DN32 8 D6
Abbey Pk Rd. DN32 8 D6
Abbey Rd. DN32 8 D6
Abbey Wk. DN31 4 C3
Abbotsway. DN32 8 D6
Abbotts Grange. DN36 18 A4
Achille Rd. DN34 13 F1
Acklam Gro. DN32 9 G6
Acorn Ct. DN35 11 B7
Adam Smith St. DN31 8 D3
Adams Rd. DN35 10 B3
Adelphi Ct. DN36 17 G3
Adelphi Dri. DN33 16 D2
Adlard Gro. DN36 18 D4
Africa Clo. DN34 13 F3
Ainslie St. DN32 9 E6
Airedale Way. DN31 4 A1
Ajax Clo. DN34 13 F3
Albatross Dri. DN37 7 E5
Albert Rd. DN35 10 D4
Albert St East. DN32 9 F3
Albert St West. DN32 9 F3
Albery Way. DN36 17 G3
Albertine Ct. DN37 16 B4
Albion St. DN32 4 F1
Alder Vw. DN33 14 A3
Alderley Edge. DN37 16 A5
Aldred Gdns. DN33 14 B5
Aldrich Rd. DN35 11 D6
Aldwych Croft. DN36 17 G3
Alexandra Rd. DN31 4 B2
Alexandra Rd. DN35 10 D3
Alfred St. DN31 4 B1
Alfred Ter. DN32 8 D6
Algernon St. DN32 15 F2
Allenby Av. DN34 8 B6
Allestree Dri. DN33 16 C2
Altoft Clo. DN37 12 B5
Altyre Way. DN36 11 A8
Alvingham Av. DN35 11 D6
Amcotts Rd. DN33 14 B4
Amesbury Av. DN33 16 C2
Amethyst Ct. DN36 17 H2
Amos Clo. DN33 16 C2
Ampleforth Av. DN37 7 H5
Ancaster Av. DN33 16 C1
Anderby Dri. DN37 7 F5
Anderson St. DN31 4 A3
Ann Gro. DN35 11 B6
Annesly St. DN31 8 D4
Anningson La. DN36 17 G2
Antrim Way. DN33 14 D5
Applegarth Clo. DN35 11 B5
Appletree Ct. DN37 6 B3
Archer Rd. DN37 16 B5
Arden Village. DN35 11 D8
Ariston St. DN32 9 H5
Armstrong Pl East. DN31 8 C3
Armstrong Pl West. DN31 8 C3
Armstrong St. DN31 8 C3
Arthur St. DN31 8 C5
Arundel Pl. DN35 11 C5
Arundel Wk. DN34 8 A5
Ascot Rd. DN37 16 B5
Asgard Way. DN33 14 C4
Ash Ct. DN35 11 B7
Ashbourne. DN37 16 A5
Ashby Clo, Great Coates. DN37 7 F4
Ashby Clo, Holton le Clay. DN36 19 G6
Ashby Rd. DN35 11 B6
Ashleigh Ct. DN37 6 C2
Ashridge Dri. DN35 11 A5
Ashtree Av. DN34 8 A6
Ashwood Dri. DN36 19 E2
Aspen Ct. DN35 11 C7
Asphodel Clo. DN36 17 H2
Athenian Way. DN37 7 G2
Atkinson La. DN37 16 C5
Auckland Rd. DN31 9 F2
Augusta Clo. DN34 14 C1
Augusta Oaks. DN34 14 C1
Augusta St. DN34 8 C6
Austin Garth. DN37 12 B4
Aylesby Gdns. DN33 14 B3
Aylesby Gro. DN33 14 B3
Aylesby La. DN37 6 B5
Aylesby Rd. DN37 7 E5
Ayscough St. DN31 4 A1

Bader Clo. DN37 7 G4
Balder Ct. DN33 14 C5
Balmoral Av. DN34 8 B5
Balmoral Rd. DN35 11 A5
Barbara Clo. DN33 16 C2
Barbican Way. DN36 17 G3
Barcroft St. DN35 10 A2
Bardney Gdns. DN34 13 H2
Bargate. DN34 8 D6
Bargate Av. DN32 14 D2
Bargate Ct. DN32 14 D1
Bark St. DN35 10 D4
Barkhouse Clo. DN35 10 E4
Barkhouse La. DN35 10 D4
Barkworth Ct. DN37 16 A5
Barmouth Dri. DN37 7 G4
Barnet Dri. DN37 17 H2
Barnett Pl. DN35 10 A2
Barnoldby Rd. DN37 16 A5
Baron Av. DN36 17 H2
Baroness Ct. DN34 8 A6
Baroness Rd. DN34 8 A6
Barry Av. DN34 13 H3
Bassett Rd. DN35 11 E5
Bath St. DN32 9 G3
Baxtergate. DN31 4 B3
Baxtergate Sq. DN31 4 B3
Bayons Av. DN33 16 C1
Bayswater Pl. DN33 16 C1
Baytree Av. DN34 8 A6
Beacon Av. DN35 10 B4
Beacon Ct. DN32 10 B4
Beaconthorpe Rd. DN35 10 C3
Beatty Av. DN33 16 D2
Beaufort Cres. DN35 11 B7
Beaumonde. DN36 19 E5
Beck Wk. DN35 11 C8
Beckhythe Clo. DN33 15 E5
Beckside Clo. DN35 11 C8
Bedale Pl. DN35 11 C7
Bedford Rd. DN35 11 E8
Bedford St. DN32 9 G4
Beech Av. DN33 14 D4
Beech Gro. DN36 19 G6
Beech Way. DN35 11 B7
Beechfield Ct. DN34 8 C6
Beechwood Av. DN33 14 A3
Beeley Rd. DN32 10 A4
Beesby Dri. DN35 11 D6
Beeson Gro. DN31 8 C4
Beeson St. DN31 8 C4
Belgrave Rd. DN33 14 B4
Belleisle Rd. DN34 13 F2
Belmont. DN36 19 F5
Belmont Clo. DN35 11 B6
Belraith Mews. DN37 16 B5
Belton Gro. DN33 14 A3
Belvoir Pk Wk. DN35 11 B7
Belvoir Rd. DN35 11 B7
Bempton Gro. DN32 15 G2
Bemrose Way. DN31 8 C5
Bennett Rd. DN35 10 B2
Bentley St. DN35 10 B4
Berkeley Rd. DN35 11 E8
Berners Rd. DN35 11 F8
Bestall Rd. DN32 10 B4
Bethlehem St. DN31 4 B4
Beverley Clo. DN36 19 F6
Beverley Ct. DN37 6 C2
Beverley Cres. DN32 15 G2
Billinghay Ct. DN35 11 D6
Binbrook Way. DN37 7 G4
Birch Av. DN34 8 B6
Birchin Way. DN31 8 C3
Birkdale. DN37 16 A5
Bishops Wk. DN34 8 C6
Bishopthorpe Rd. DN35 11 D6
Blackthorn Dri. DN37 7 F4
Blakeney Lea. DN35 11 D8
Blaydon Gro. DN34 13 G2
Blenheim Pl. DN35 11 C5
Blundell Av. DN35 10 A2
Bodiam Way. DN32 4 E2
Bolingbroke Rd. DN35 11 E6
Bonby Gro. DN33 14 A3
Boulevard Av. DN31 8 B5
Boundary Rd. DN33 16 C3
Bowers Av. DN31 8 B5
Bowfield Clo. DN37 7 F4
Bowling Green La. DN32 4 D3
Bowling Green Way. DN32 4 D3
Bowling La. DN35 10 C4
Bracken Pk. DN33 16 C1
Bracken Pl. DN37 7 F6
Bradford Av. DN35 11 D5
Bradley Rd. DN37 13 G3
Bradley St. DN32 4 E2
Bradman Ct. DN32 9 G3
Braemar Rd. DN35 11 C6
Braeton La. DN33 17 E2
Bramble Way. DN35 11 C8
Bramhall St. DN35 10 B2
Brampton Way. DN35 11 B6
Bransdale Way. DN37 7 G5
Brax Clo. DN33 14 B5
Bremerhaven Way. DN33 14 A3
Brereton Av. DN35 10 A2
Brewery St. DN31 4 B3
Brian Av, Cleethorpes. DN35 11 A6
Brian Av, Waltham. DN37 16 B5
Briar La, Scartho. DN33 16 B1
Briar La, Healing. DN37 6 B3
Bridge St Nth. DN32 9 F3
Brighowgate. DN32 8 D6
Brighton St. DN35 10 E4
Brigsley Rd. DN37 16 B6
Britannia Cres. DN34 13 F1
Brixham Ct. DN33 16 C3
Broadfield Rd. DN33 14 B6
Broadway. DN34 13 F2
Brock Clo. DN33 14 C3
Brocklesby Pl. DN34 13 H2
Brocklesby Rd. DN34 13 G3
Bronzegarth. DN32 15 G2
Brookfield Rd. DN33 16 B1
Brooklands Av. DN35 11 E5
Brooklyn Dri. DN36 19 F1
Broughton Dri. DN35 11 D8
Browns Orchard. DN32 8 D6
Brunton Way. DN36 17 H4
Buck Beck Way. DN35 11 B8
Buckfast Clo. DN37 7 G4
Buckingham Gro. DN33 14 B5
Bude Clo. DN36 17 G2
Bull Ring La. DN31 4 B3
Buller St. DN32 9 F5
Bullfinch La. DN35 11 C8
Bulwick Av. DN33 16 C2
Burcom Av. DN36 19 E2
Burley Av. DN35 11 D6
Burnham Reach. DN35 11 D8
Burns Gro. DN33 14 C3
Bursar St. DN35 10 C4
Burwell Dri. DN33 14 B3
Butler Pl. DN35 9 H5
Butt La. DN37 12 A3
Butterfield Clo. DN37 12 B4
Buttermere Cres. DN36 18 C2
Buttermere Way. DN32 4 F2
Butterwick Clo. DN35 11 D6
Byland Gro. DN37 7 G3
Byron Gro. DN33 14 C3
Bywood Pl. DN37 7 F6

Cabourne Rd. DN33 14 B4
Caenby Rd, DN35 11 D6
Caistor Dri. DN33 14 B4
Caistor Rd. DN37 12 A6
Calver Cres. DN37 7 G5
Camargue Av. DN37 16 D5
Cambrian Way. DN36 19 F4
Cambridge Ct. DN34 13 H1
Cambridge Rd. DN34 13 H1
Cambridge St. DN35 10 D4
Campbell Gro. DN37 7 G4
Campden Cres. DN35 10 B3
Campions Clo. DN36 19 F5
Candlesby Rd. DN37 7 E5
Canon Oakes Ct. DN36 18 A4
Canterbury Dri. DN34 8 C6
Carbis Clo. DN36 17 G3
Cardiff Av. DN36 17 G3
Cardinal Ct. DN37 16 A4
Carisbrooke Clo. DN36 17 H2
Carlton Av. DN37 6 B3
Carlton Clo. DN35 11 F8
Carlton Rd, Grimsby. DN34 8 C6
Carlton Rd, Healing. DN37 6 B2
Carlyle Clo. DN35 11 E8
Carmen Cres. DN36 19 F4
Carnaby Gro. DN32 15 G1
Carnavon Av. DN34 14 C2
Carnforth Cres. DN34 14 A2
Carnoustie. DN37 16 A5
Carr La, Grimsby. DN35 9 H5
Carr La, Healing. DN37 6 C4
Carrick La. DN36 17 G3
Carrington Dri. DN36 19 E1
Carson Av. DN34 8 B6
Cartergate. DN31 4 A4
Cartledge Av. DN32 9 G6
Cartmel Gro. DN32 9 H6
Casswell Clo. DN32 9 G4
Castle St. DN32 9 G4
Castleford Av. DN34 14 A2
Catherine St. DN31 4 D4
Cattistock Rd. DN35 11 C7
Cavendish Clo. DN35 11 F8
Cavendish Way. DN32 4 F3
Cedar Clo. DN35 11 B7
Cemetery Cres. DN37 12 A5
Cemetery Rd. DN37 12 A5
Central Par. DN34 8 A6
Central Prom. DN35 10 D3
Chadwell Springs. DN37 16 A5
Chaffinch Dri. DN35 11 C8
Chandlers Clo. DN36 17 F2
Chantry La. DN31 8 C5
Chapman Ct. DN31 4 A1
Chapman Cres. DN36 19 E2
Chapman Gro. DN35 10 D4
Chapman Rd. DN35 10 B2
Charles Av, Laceby. DN37 12 A5
Charles Av, New Waltham. DN36 17 G3
Charles Av, Scartho. DN33 14 D5
Charles Hume Ct. DN32 9 H4
Charles St. DN35 10 D4
Charlton St. DN31 8 C4
Chatsworth Pl. DN35 11 A5
Cheapside. DN37 16 C5
Cheesemans Clo. DN37 16 C5
Cheesemans La. DN37 16 C5
Chelmsford Av. DN34 8 B6
Chelmsford Pl. DN34 8 B6
Chelsea Wk. DN35 11 E8
Cheltenham Way. DN35 11 D8
Chepstow Gro. DN34 14 A2
Cherry Dale. DN35 11 B6
Cherry Tree Cres. DN34 7 H6
Cheshire Wk. DN37 7 G4
Chester Grange. DN33 15 E5
Chester Pl. DN35 11 A5
Chester Wk. DN34 14 A2
Chestnut Av. DN31 8 C5
Chestnut Clo. DN37 16 A6
Chestnut Rd. DN37 16 A5
Chestnut Wk. DN37 6 D3
Chichester Rd. DN35 11 D6
Chiltern Dri. DN37 16 B6
Chiltern Way. DN33 16 D
Chingford Av. DN34 14 A
Chippendale Clo. DN36 18 D
Christine Pl. DN33 17 E
Church Av. DN36 18 D
Church Clo. DN32 15 H
Church La, Bradley. DN37 13 G4
Church La, Grimsby. DN31 4 B4
Church La, Holton le Clay. DN36 19 F5
Church La, Humberston. DN36 19 E3
Church La, Laceby. DN37 12 B5
Church La, Scartho. DN33 14 D5
Church La, Waltham. DN37 16 C5
Church La, Weelsby. DN32 15 H1
Church St. DN32 9 F3
Church Vw, Grimsby. DN34 7 G6
Church Vw, Waltham. DN37 16 C5
Church Wk. DN36 19 F5
Churchill Way. DN32 4 F3
Clare Ct. DN34 14 A1
Claremont Rd. DN32 10 B4
Clarendon Rd. DN34 13 G3
Clark Av. DN31 8 B5
Clavering St. DN31 8 B3
Clay La. DN36 19 F4
Claymore Clo. DN35 10 C4
Clayton Wk. DN31 4 B3
Clee Cres. DN32 10 A4
Clee Fields Clo. DN32 15 H2
Clee Rd. DN32 10 A4
Clee Village. DN32 10 A4
Cleeness Dri. DN36 19 E1
Cleethorpes Chalet Pk. DN36 19 H2
Cleethorpe Rd. DN31 9 E3
Clerke St. DN35 9 H4
Cleveland St. DN31 8 B3
Clifton Rd. DN34 8 B6
Clixby Clo. DN35 11 E6
Clumber Pl. DN35 11 C5
Colin Av. DN32 9 H6
College Av. DN33 16 D1
College Gdns. DN33 16 D1
College St, Cleethorpes. DN35 10 C3
College St, Grimsby. DN34 8 C6
Collingwood Cres. DN34 13 F3
Colson Pl. DN35 9 H5
Coltsfoot Dri. DN37 16 A5
Columbia Rd. DN32 9 G6
Columbus Way. DN33 13 H4
Combe St. DN35 10 A2
Comber Pl. DN32 9 F4
Compton Dri. DN34 8 C6
Coningsby Dri. DN34 14 B2
Coniston Av. DN33 16 B2
Coniston Cres. DN36 18 C2
Connaught Av. DN32 14 D2
Connisborough Av. DN36 17 F3
Convamore Rd. DN32 4 F3
Conway Av. DN34 8 A5
Conyard Rd. DN35 10 C3
Conyers Av. DN33 14 D5
Cooks La. DN37 7 F3
Cooper La. DN37 12 A4
Cooper Rd. DN32 9 G6
Coppergate. DN37 12 A6
Coral Dri. DN37 16 B4
Corinthian Av. DN34 8 B6
Cormorant Dri. DN37 7 E5
Cornfield Clo. DN33 16 B1
Cornwell Clo. DN33 14 C3
Coronation Rd. DN35 10 D4
Corporation Rd. DN31 4 A1
Cosgrove St. DN35 10 D3
Cotswold Dri. DN37 16 B6

ottage Yard La. DN36 18 D4
ottages Plot. DN37 13 F3
ottesmore Rd. DN35 11 C7
oulam Pl. DN36 19 E2
oulbeck Dri. DN35 11 B5
oventry Av. DN34 14 A1
ragston Av. DN33 14 D4
raithie Rd. DN35 11 C5
rake Av. DN33 14 C5
rampin Rd. DN35 10 C3
ranbourne Clo. DN35 11 D8
ranwell Dri. DN37 7 H4
raven Rd. DN35 9 H5
rescent St. DN31 4 A3
ressy St. DN31 9 E3
ridling Pl. DN35 11 B5
rofters Gro. DN36 17 G4
romer Av. DN34 14 A2
romwell Rd, Cleethorpes. DN35 11 E5
romwell Rd, Great Coates. DN37 7 G3
romwell Rd, Grimsby. DN31 8 A4
rosby Rd. DN33 14 A4
rosland Rd. DN37 7 F4
ross Coates Rd. DN34 8 B6
Cross La, Pinfold La. DN33 14 D6
ross St, Cleethorpes. DN35 10 C3
ross St, Grimsby. DN31 9 F2
ross St, Waltham. DN37 16 C5
row Hill Av. DN35 10 C4
rowland Av. DN34 13 H2
rowle Dri. DN33 14 A4
roxby Av. DN33 16 D1
roxby Gro. DN33 16 D2
umberland Av. DN32 14 D2
umberland Rd. DN35 11 E8
urry Rd. DN34 7 H6
urzon Av. DN35 11 B5
urzon Ct. DN35 11 B5
uttleby. DN35 10 D4
ynthia Rd. DN32 10 A4
yrano Way. DN37 7 E5
Cyril Cooper Ct, Abbey Dri East. DN32 8 D6

Daggett Rd. DN35 11 E6
Dale Vw. DN33 14 A4
Dame Kendal Gro. DN33 14 C3
Danesfield Av. DN37 16 C4
Darwin Ct. DN34 13 H1
Daubney St. DN35 10 A2
Davenport Dri. DN35 11 A5
David Pl. DN36 17 G4
David St. DN32 15 F1
Davie Pl. DN35 9 H5
Davisons Av. DN31 4 B1
Dawlish Rd. DN33 16 D3
Deansgate. DN31 4 A4
Deaton La. DN36 17 G3
Deene Clo. DN34 13 F3
Defender Dri. DN37 7 E5
Delamere Ct. DN35 11 D8
Denby Dri. DN35 11 A6
Dene Rd. DN32 15 E2
Derry Way. DN33 16 C1
Derwent Dri. DN36 18 C1
Devonshire Av. DN32 14 D2
Dial Sq. DN31 4 C3
Digby Gdns. DN34 14 A2
Dixon Av. DN32 15 E2
Dolby Vale. DN33 14 A3
Dolphin St. DN35 10 D3
Dominion Ct. DN36 17 G3
Donnington St. DN32 4 F4
Dorothy Av. DN37 16 C4
Doughty Clo. DN37 16 C4
Doughty Rd. DN32 4 C3
Douglas Av. DN31 8 B5
Douglas Rd. DN35 10 B2
Dovedale Dri. DN33 16 D2
Dover St. DN31 4 A2
Downing Clo. DN34 13 H1
Drake Av. DN32 15 H1
Drew Av. DN32 15 F3
Drury Clo. DN37 16 A5
Drury La. DN36 17 G3
Duchess St. DN32 4 B4
Dudley Pl. DN35 11 B5
Dudley St. DN31 8 C5
Dugard Rd. DN35 9 H5
Duke St. DN32 9 G4
Dunbar Av. DN36 17 F3
Duncombe Gdns. DN32 4 E1
Duncombe St. DN32 4 E1
Dunmow St. DN31 8 C4
Durban Rd. DN32 9 G5
Durham Av. DN34 8 A5
Durham Rd. DN35 11 A5
Dursley Av. DN36 17 F3
Dymoke Dri. DN37 7 F6

Earl Av. DN36 17 H2
Earl St. DN31 4 A3
Eason Rd. DN33 14 C5
East End Clo. DN33 15 E5
East Gate. DN32 4 D2
East Marsh St. DN31 4 D2
East St Marys Gate. DN31 4 B3
East St. DN31 4 D3
Eastbourne Way. DN33 16 D2
Eastern Inway. DN34 14 A2
Eastfield. DN36 19 E2
Eastfield Av. DN33 17 E2
Eastfield Rise. DN36 19 F5
Eastside Rd. DN31 9 F3
Eastville Rd. DN33 14 A4
Eastwood Av. DN34 14 D2
Eaton Ct. DN34 14 C1
Edge Av. DN33 14 D4
Edinburgh Dri. DN36 19 E4
Edmonds Way. DN31 4 B2
Edward St, Cleethorpes. DN35 10 C4
Edward St, Grimsby. DN32 4 E4
Egton Way. DN37 7 G4
Elderberry Way. DN35 11 B7
Eleanor St. DN32 4 E2
Elizabeth Clo. DN33 16 C2
Ellesmere Rise. DN34 13 F3
Ellis Way. DN31 4 D2
Elliston St. DN35 10 A2
Elm Av, Cleethorpes. DN35 10 C4
Elm Av, Grimsby. DN34 8 A6
Elm Gro. DN37 6 C3
Elm La. DN37 12 A6
Elm Rd, Cleethorpes. DN35 10 C4
Elm Rd, Waltham. DN37 16 C6
Elsenham Rd. DN31 8 B3
Elsham Dri. DN37 16 B6
Elsham Gro. DN33 14 B3
Elwyn Pl. DN35 11 B7
Emfield Gro. DN33 16 C3
Emfield Rd. DN33 16 B2
Enfield Av. DN36 17 H3
Ennerdale Clo. DN36 18 C2
Enterprise Way. DN32 9 G6
Escart Rd. DN32 9 H6
Eskdale Way. DN37 7 F4
Eskham Clo. DN35 11 D6
Estate Rd No. 1. DN31 7 H2
Estate Rd No. 2. DN31 7 H3
Estate Rd No. 3. DN31 7 H2
Estate Rd No. 4. DN31 7 H2
Estate Rd No. 5. DN31 7 H2
Estate Rd No. 6. DN31 7 H2
Estate Rd No. 7. DN31 7 H3
Estuary Way. DN31 8 B2
Evelyn Gro Nth. DN32 9 H6
Evelyn Gro Sth. DN32 9 H6
Evendine Ct. DN36 19 G6
Evesham Av. DN34 13 G2
Exeter Ct. DN34 13 F3

Fair View Av. DN35 10 C4
Fairfax Rd. DN34 8 B5
Fairfield Av. DN33 16 C2
Fairfield Ct. DN35 11 E8
Fairfield Rd. DN33 16 C2
Fairmont Rd. DN32 9 G6
Fairway. DN37 16 C5
Fairway Ct. DN35 19 F1
Fairways. DN35 11 E8
Fallowfield Rd. DN33 16 B2
Farebrother St. DN32 15 E1
Faringdon Rd. DN31 9 G2
Farmhouse Mews. DN36 17 G3
Fauconberg Av. DN33 14 C5
Faulding Way. DN37 7 E5
Fearn Clo. DN36 17 H3
Felstead Rd. DN34 7 H6
Fenby Clo. DN37 7 F6
Fenwick Ct. DN36 19 F6
Ferndale Way. DN31 4 B1
Ferndown. DN37 7 G3
Fernhill. DN37 7 F6
Fernie Pl. DN35 11 C7
Ferriby La. DN33 14 C5
Field Clo. DN37 12 B5
Field Head Rd. DN37 12 A5
Fieldhouse Rd. DN36 19 E1
Fildes St. DN31 4 B2
Filey Rd. DN32 15 G2
Fillingham Cres. DN35 11 D6
Findlay Cres. DN36 17 H3
Finsbury Dri. DN33 14 B5
Fircroft Way. DN34 8 B5
Firsby Cres. DN33 14 A4
First Av. DN33 14 C2
Fish Dock Rd. DN31 9 F3
Fisher Pl. DN35 10 B3
Fishermans Wharf. DN31 4 B2
Fiskerton Clo. DN34 13 H2
Fiskerton Way. DN37 7 G1
Fitzwilliam Mews. DN35 11 C7
Fleetwood Clo. DN33 16 C2
Fletcher Rd. DN34 7 H6
Fletchers Yd. DN32 4 B4
Florence St. DN32 15 E1
Flottergate Mall. DN31 4 B3
Flour Sq. DN31 9 E3
Fords Av. DN37 6 C3
Forest Dri. DN36 19 F2
Forest Way. DN36 19 F2
Forge Way. DN36 19 F4
Forsythia Rise. DN33 14 C5
Fortuna Way. DN37 7 E5
Fotheaby St. DN31 4 D1
Fountain Clo. DN37 16 B4
Fountains Av. DN37 7 G4
Foxglove Gdns. DN34 13 H1
Foxhill. DN37 7 F6
Frankland Pl. DN35 10 B2
Fraser St. DN32 4 F3
Frederick St, Cleethorpes. DN35 10 C3
Frederick St, Grimsby. DN31 4 A1
Frederick Ward Way. DN31 4 A3
Freeman Ct. DN36 19 G5
Freeman St. DN32 4 E2
Freeston St. DN35 9 H5
Freyja Croft. DN33 14 B4
Freshney Dri. DN31 4 A1
Friargate. DN31 4 B3
Friargate Sq. DN31 4 B3
Friary Wk. DN31 4 B3
Frobisher Av. DN32 15 H1
Frusher Av. DN33 14 D3
Fulham Pk. DN33 14 B4
Fuller St. DN35 10 B2
Fulstow Gro. DN33 14 B4

Garbutt Pl. DN35 11 E5
Garden Dri. DN36 17 G2
Garden St. DN32 4 B4
Garibaldi St. DN32 4 E1
Garner St. DN32 15 E1
Garnett St. DN35 10 B2
Garrick La. DN36 17 G2
Garth La. DN31 4 B2
Garthway. DN36 19 F6
Garton Gro. DN32 15 G2
Gate La. DN33 14 D6
Gate Way. DN31 8 C2
Gayton Rd. DN35 11 E6
Gedney Clo. DN37 7 F5
George Janney Ct. DN32 9 F4
George St. DN35 10 D4
Georges St. DN31 4 C3
Gertrude St. DN32 15 E2
Gibraltar La. DN37 12 A4
Gilbey Rd. DN31 8 B3
Giles St. DN35 10 C4
Gill Ct. DN33 14 B5
Girton Rd. DN34 13 H1
Glebe Clo, Holton le Clay. DN36 19 F4
Glebe Clo, Humberston. DN36 18 D4
Glebe Rd, Cleethorpes. DN35 10 D4
Glebe Rd, Humberston. DN36 18 D3
Glebe Rd, Scartho. DN33 15 E5
Gleneagles. DN37 16 A5
Glenfield Rd. DN37 7 F4
Gloria Way. DN37 7 E5
Gloucester Av. DN34 14 B2
Goldgarth. DN32 15 G2
Goring Pl. DN35 10 B3
Gorton St. DN31 9 F2
Gosport Rd. DN34 8 A6
Goxhill Gdns. DN34 13 H2
Grafton St. DN32 9 G3
Grainsby Av, Cleethorpes. DN35 11 B6
Grainsby Av, Holton le Clay. DN36 19 G6
Grampian Way. DN33 16 C1
Grange Av. DN37 12 B5
Grange Farm La. DN36 17 H3
Grange Wk. DN34 8 A6
Grant St. DN35 10 C3
Grantham Av. DN33 14 D5
Granville St. DN32 15 F1
Grasby Cres. DN37 7 F5
Grasmere Gro. DN36 18 C2
Grayling Clo. DN37 7 G5
Great Coates Rd, Gt Coates. DN37 7 E4
Great Coates Rd, Healing. DN37 6 B3
Green Hill. DN35 11 B6
Greenfinch Dri. DN35 11 C8
Greenlands Av. DN36 17 G3
Greenway. DN37 16 D6
Greethams La. DN32 10 A4
Grey Friars. DN37 7 F5
Grime St. DN31 4 D2
Grimsby Rd, Cleethorpes. DN35 10 A1
Grimsby Rd, Humberston. DN36 11 B7
Grimsby Rd, Laceby. DN37 12 B5
Grimsby Rd, Waltham. DN37 16 D4
Grosvenor Ct. DN35 11 E8
Grosvenor Cres. DN32 4 A4
Grosvenor St. DN32 4 A4
Grove Cres, DN32 10 A3
Grove La. DN37 16 C6
Guildford St. DN32 9 G4
Gunby Pl. DN35 11 C5
Gunners Way. DN34 13 F2

Haigh St. DN35 10 E4
Haile Rd. DN36 19 E1
Hainton Av. DN32 4 E4
Halton Pl. DN35 11 B6
Halton Way. DN34 14 B2
Hamilton Clo. DN34 13 F2
Hamilton St. DN32 9 G3
Hamont Rd. DN32 10 A3
Hampstead Pk. DN33 14 B5
Hampton Ct, Cleethorpes. DN35 11 B5
Hampton Ct, Humberston. DN35 11 D8
Hardys Rd. DN35 11 D5
Hare St. DN32 9 F6
Harewood Gro. DN35 11 D8
Hargrave St. DN31 8 C4
Harlech Way. DN32 4 E1
Harlestone Ct. DN34 13 F2
Harlow St. DN31 8 B3
Harneis Cres. DN37 12 B4
Harold St. DN32 9 G4
Harrington St. DN35 10 A1
Harrison St. DN31 8 C5
Hart St. DN35 10 A2
Harvest Cres. DN37 16 A5
Hatcliffe Clo. DN33 14 B4
Hatton Gro. DN33 14 B4
Haven Av. DN31 8 C4
Haven Gdns. DN31 8 B3
Haven Ter. DN31 4 A2
Haven Wk. DN31 4 C3
Haverstoe Pl. DN35 11 A6
Hawerby Rd. DN37 12 A4
Hawkins Gro. DN32 15 H1
Hawthorn Clo. DN37 6 B2
Hawthorne Av, Cleethorpes. DN35 10 B2
Hawthorne Av, New Waltham. DN36 17 F4
Hawthorne Av, Scartho. DN33 16 D1
Haycroft Av. DN31 8 C5
Haycroft St. DN31 8 C5
Hayling Mere. DN35 11 D8
Hays Clo. DN36 19 F5
Heatherdale Clo. DN33 16 D2
Heathfield Ct. DN34 14 C1
Heimdall Rd. DN33 14 C4
Helene Gro. DN32 10 A3
Hemswell Dri. DN37 7 H4
Heneage Rd. DN32 4 E3
Henry St. DN31 8 C4
Hereford Av. DN34 14 C2
Heritage Sq. DN31 4 C2
Heron Clo. DN32 15 H2
Heron Way. DN36 19 F4
Hewitts Av. DN36 11 A8
Hewitts Manor. DN35 11 B7
Hewson Rd. DN36 19 E2
Hey St. DN35 11 D5
Heythorp Rd. DN35 11 C7
Hibaldstow Clo. DN34 14 A2
High St, Cleethorpes. DN35 10 D3
High St, Laceby. DN37 12 B5
High St, Waltham. DN37 16 C5
High Thorpe Cres. DN35 11 B6
Highcliff Rd. DN35 10 E4
Highfield Av. DN32 15 E1
Highgate. DN35 10 D4
Hilary Rd. DN33 16 D2
Hilda St. DN32 9 G3
Hildyard St. DN32 9 G4
Hill Top Pl. DN34 13 F3
Hillary Way. DN37 7 G4
Hilton Ct. DN35 19 F1
Hinkler St. DN35 10 D4
Holles St. DN32 4 E2
Hollingsworth Clo. DN35 11 B7
Holme Av. DN36 17 G3
Holme Farm Clo. DN37 7 G3
Holme St. DN32 4 D3
Holton Ct. DN36 19 F6
Holton Mt. DN36 19 F5
Holyoake Rd. DN32 10 A4
Home Paddock. DN37 16 C5
Homefield Av. DN33 14 D3
Honeysuckle Ct. DN35 11 C8
Hope St, Cleethorpes. DN35 10 E4
Hope St, Grimsby. DN32 9 G3
Howard Gro. DN32 15 H1
Howlett Rd. DN35 11 E5
Huddleston Rd. DN32 9 G6
Humber Bank Sth. DN31 9 G2
Humber Bridge. DN31 9 G3
Humber Bridge Rd. DN31 9 G3
Humber St, Cleethorpes. DN35 10 D4
Humber St, Grimsby. DN31 9 G3
Humber Ter. DN31 4 A2
Humberston Av. DN36 18 A4
Humberston Rd, Cleethorpes. DN35 11 A5
Humberston Rd, Humberston. DN36 18 D2
Humberstone Rd. DN32 9 G5
Hume St. DN31 8 C5
Hunsley Cres. DN32 15 H3
Hunters Clo. DN37 7 E4
Hurford Pl. DN33 16 C3
Hurstlea Dri. DN36 19 E1
Hutchinson Rd. DN35 10 C2
Hutton Rd. DN31 9 F2

Imperial Av. DN35 10 A2
INDUSTRIAL & RETAIL:
Abbeygate Shopping Centre. DN31 4 B3
Acorn Business Centre. DN31 4 C4
Alexandra Retail Pk. DN31 4 C1
Birchin Way Ind Est. DN31 8 B3
Europa Business DN31 8 B2
Europark Ind Est. DN37 7 F1

Great Grimsby Business Pk. DN37 7 G2
High Point Retail Pk. DN31 9 E3
South Humberside Ind Est. DN31 7 H3
Venture Business Pk. DN31 8 B2
West Marsh Ind Est. DN31 4 B1
Ingleby Gro. DN37 7 H5
Ingram Pl. DN35 11 B7
Ings La. DN37 16 C5
Intax Farm Mews. DN32 15 F1
Iona Dri. DN36 19 F2
Irby Ct. DN35 11 B6
Isaacs Hill. DN35 10 C3
Itterby Cres. DN35 11 A6

Jackson St. DN31 4 A1
Jacksons Pl. DN36 18 B1
James St. DN31 8 C4
Janton Ct. DN36 17 G2
Jenner Pl. DN35 9 H5
Johnson St. DN35 9 H4
Joseph Ogle. DN36 17 F2
Joseph St. DN31 8 C4
Julian St. DN32 9 F5
Juniper Way. DN33 14 C5
Jutland Ct. DN36 17 H2

Kathleen Av. DN35 10 B2
Kathleen Gro. DN32 10 A3
Kaymile Clo. DN36 17 G3
Keir Hardie Wk. DN32 4 C4
Keith Cres. DN37 12 A5
Kelham Rd. DN32 10 B4
Kelstern Ct. DN34 14 A2
Kemeshame Ct. DN37 16 D5
Kemp Rd. DN31 9 G1
Kenford Ct. DN36 17 G2
Kenilworth Rd. DN35 11 B5
Kenmar Rd. DN37 12 A5
Kensington Pl. DN33 17 E1
Kent St. DN32 9 F3
Kettlewell St. DN32 15 E1
Kew Rd. DN35 10 C4
Kiddier Av. DN33 16 C2
King Edward St. DN31 9 E4
Kings Ct. DN34 14 A1
Kings Mews. DN35 19 F1
Kings Par. DN35 10 E4
Kings Rd, Cleethorpes. DN35 11 E5
Kings Rd, Humberston. DN35 19 F1
Kingsley Gro. DN33 14 C3
Kingston Av. DN34 8 B6
Kingston Clo. DN35 11 E8
Kingsway. DN35 10 E4
Kirk Gate. DN37 16 C5
Kirk Side. DN37 16 C5
Kirkstead Cres. DN33 14 B4
Kirmington Gdns. DN34 8 A6
Knight St. DN32 9 H6
Knights Clo. DN37 12 B5
Knightsbridge. DN36 17 G3
Knoll St. DN35 10 D4
Konigswinter Ct. DN36 17 G3
Kymer Pl. DN35 11 E5

Laburnum Av. DN37 16 B5
Laburnum Clo. DN37 16 B5
Laburnum Dri. DN34 7 G6
Laceby Rd. DN34 13 F3
Lady Frances Cres. DN35 10 A4
Ladysmith Rd. DN32 9 F5
Laforey Rd. DN37 7 G2
Lairgate Pl. DN35 11 D8
Lambert Rd. DN32 14 D1
Lambourne Ct. DN35 11 D8
Lampton Gro. DN32 15 E1
Lancaster Av. DN31 8 C5
Lancaster Ct. DN33 14 B5
Lancaster Gate. DN36 19 F6
Lancing Way. DN33 16 C1
Landeck Av. DN34 8 B6
Langdale Av. DN33 16 B2
Langley Pl. DN35 11 E6
Langton Clo. DN33 14 B4
Langton Dri. DN33 14 B3
Langton Rd. DN36 19 G6
Lansdown Link. DN35 11 C6
Lansdowne Av. DN32 14 D3
Larch Rd. DN35 11 B7
Larden Av. DN33 16 C2
Larmour Rd. DN37 7 F4
Laurel Clo. DN33 14 C4
Lavenham Rd. DN33 16 B1
Lawrence St. DN31 8 C4
Lawson Av. DN31 8 C5
Leas Clo. DN37 16 C4
Ledbury Dri. DN36 17 H2
Legsby Av. DN32 15 E1
Legsby Pl. DN32 15 E2
Leighton Gro. DN33 14 C3
Lestrange St. DN35 10 A3
Lewis Rd. DN35 10 B2
Lichfield Rd. DN32 9 H6
Lidgard Rd. DN36 19 E2
Limber Ct. DN34 8 A6
Limber Vale. DN34 8 A6
Lime Gro, Holton le Clay. DN36 19 F6
Lime Gro, Humberston. DN36 18 D4
Lime St. DN31 8 C5
Limetree Av. DN33 14 D4
Lincoln Av. DN31 8 C5
Lincoln Rd. DN35 11 A5
Lindisfarne Av. DN36 17 F3
Lindrick Wk. DN37 16 A5
Lindsey Dri, Healing. DN37 6 C3
Lindsey Dri, Humberston. DN36 19 E4
Lindsey Rise. DN33 16 D1
Lindsey Rd. DN35 11 D5
Lindum Rd. DN35 11 D5
Links Rd. DN35 11 E6
Linwood Av. DN33 16 D1
Lisburn Gro. DN33 14 D4
Lister St. DN31 8 C4
Little Coates Rd. DN34 13 G3
Little Michael St. DN34 8 C5
Littlebeck Rd. DN36 18 C2
Littlefield La. DN34 8 B6
Lock Hill. DN31 9 E3
Loft Av. DN37 7 H4
Lombard St. DN34 8 B5
Lomond Gro. DN36 18 C2
Longfield Rd. DN34 13 G2
Longhorn Clo. DN37 16 A5
Longmeadows Dri. DN37 12 B4
Lonsdale Clo. DN36 18 D4
Lopham La. DN37 12 A6
Lord St. DN31 8 C4
Louth Rd, Holton le Clay. DN36 19 E4
Louth Rd, New Waltham. DN36 17 F4
Louth Rd, Scartho. DN33 16 D1
Loveden Ct. DN35 11 E6
Lovett St. DN35 10 A2
Low Rd. DN37 6 B3
Lower Burgess St. DN31 4 D1
Lower Spring St. DN31 9 E3
Lucas Ct. DN37 6 B2
Ludborough Way. DN35 11 D6
Ludford St. DN32 9 E6
Ludgate Clo. DN37 16 C5
Ludlow Av. DN34 8 A5
Ludlow Pl. DN35 11 C5
Lyndhurst Av. DN33 14 D4
Lynton Rise. DN35 11 C6
Lytham Dri. DN37 16 B6

Macaulay St. DN31 8 C5
Maclure St. DN31 9 F2
McVeigh Ct. DN37 6 C3
Magdalene Rd. DN34 14 A1
Magnolia Dri. DN36 19 G6
Maidwell Way. DN34 13 E2
Malcolm Rd. DN34 13 H3
Mallard Clo. DN37 6 B3
Mallard Mews. DN32 9 E6
Malmesbury Dri. DN34 8 C6
Maltby Av. DN37 13 E3
Maltings Way. DN31 9 E4
Malvern Av. DN33 14 A3
Manchester St. DN35 10 B2
Mandela Link. DN31 8 C5
Manley Gdns. DN35 11 E6
Manningtree Clo. DN32 9 E6
Manor Av. DN32 4 B4
Manor Ct. DN32 4 B4
Manor Dri. DN37 16 C4
Mansel St. DN32 9 H4
Manson Clo. DN34 13 F3
Maple Av. DN34 7 G6
Maple Gro, Healing. DN37 6 C3
Maple Gro, New Waltham. DN36 17 F4
Marcus St. DN34 8 A6
Margaret Pl. DN36 17 G3
Margaret St. DN32 4 E4
Marian Way. DN37 16 A5
Marigold Wk. DN35 11 C8
Market Sq. DN31 4 B3
Market St, Grimsby. DN31 4 D1
Market St, Cleethorpes. DN35 10 D3
Markham Mews. DN37 16 D5
Markhams Orchard. DN33 16 D2
Marklew Av. DN34 8 B5
Marlborough Way. DN35 11 D8
Marples Mws. DN35 10 E4
Marquis Av. DN36 17 H2
Marsden Rd. DN31 9 G3
Marsh Chapel Clo. DN35 11 D6
Marshall Av. DN34 8 B6
Martin Way. DN36 17 F3
Marton Gro. DN33 14 A4
Martyn Rd. DN35 10 B3
Marylebone Wk. DN33 14 B4
Mathews St. DN35 10 A2
Matlock Dri. DN37 7 H4
Maxwell Ct. DN34 13 F2
May St. DN35 10 B2
Mayfair Ct. DN35 11 E8
Mayfair Cres. DN37 16 B5
Mayfair Dri East. DN37 7 F5
Mayfair Dri West. DN37 7 F5
Mayfield Clo. DN33 16 B1
Meadow Ct. DN34 7 G6
Meadow Croft. DN37 16 C5
Meadow Dri, Healing. DN37 6 C2
Meadow Dri, Scartho. DN33 16 B1
Meadow Vw. DN35 11 D8
Meadowbank. DN37 7 F4
Medway Pl. DN34 14 A2
Melbourne Av. DN33 14 D4
Melrose Way. DN37 7 G4
Mendip Av. DN33 16 C1
Mersey Way. DN37 7 G4
Middle Ct. DN31 4 D2
Middle Thorpe Rd. DN35 11 B6
Midfield Pl. DN36 19 E3
Midfield Rd. DN36 18 D3
Mill Av. DN31 8 C4
Mill Clo. DN37 16 C6
Mill Garth. DN35 11 B7
Mill Hill Cres. DN35 10 C4
Mill Pl. DN35 10 D3
Mill Rd. DN35 10 C4
Mill Vw. DN37 16 C5
Miller Av. DN32 10 A3
Millfield Av. DN33 14 D4
Millom Way. DN32 4 F1
Milton Rd. DN33 14 B3
Minnow Ct. DN37 7 G5
Minshull Rd. DN35 11 D6
Mirfield Rd. DN32 15 F2
Mollison Av. DN35 10 D4
Montague St. DN35 9 H4
Montgomery Rd. DN35 10 B4
Moody La. DN31 7 H1
Moorland Dri. DN36 17 G2
Mordaunt Av. DN33 16 C2
Morgan Way. DN35 10 C4
Morpeth Wk. DN34 8 A6
Morton Rd. DN34 8 B5
Moss Rd. DN32 4 C4
Moulton Clo. DN34 13 F2
Mount Pleasant. DN36 19 F6
Mount Pleasant. DN37 16 C4
Muirfield. DN37 16 A5
Mulgrave Clo. DN37 7 H4
Murray St. DN31 9 F3
Myfarm Ct. DN37 6 B3

Nacton St. DN31 9 F3
Nairn Way. DN34 14 C1
Naseby Dri. DN31 8 B5
Naseby Gro. DN31 8 B5
Nelson St. DN32 9 F3
Nelson Way. DN34 13 F2
Neptune St. DN35 10 C2
Neville St. DN35 10 B2
Neville Turner Way. DN37 16 B5
New Biggin Wk. DN31 4 B3
New Cartergate. DN31 4 A3
New Chapel La. DN37 12 B5
New Clo. DN33 14 C3
New Haven Ter. DN31 8 B3
New Rd, Cleethorpes. DN35 10 D4
New Rd, Laceby. DN37 12 C5
New Rd, Waltham. DN37 16 C5
New St. DN31 4 C3
Newbury Av. DN37 7 G3
Newbury Gro. DN34 13 G2
Newbury Ter. DN37 7 G3
Newby Rd. DN31 8 C5
Newlands Pk. DN36 19 F1
Newlyn Clo. DN36 17 G2
Newmarch Ct. DN33 14 C5
Newmarch Cres. DN33 14 D6
Newmarket St. DN32 4 E1
Newsham Dri. DN34 8 A6
Newstead Av. DN36 19 G5
Newstead Rd. DN35 11 C5
Newton Gro. DN33 14 C3
Nicholson Rd. DN37 6 C2
Nicholson St. DN35 11 D5
Norfolk La. DN35 10 C3
Norman Rd. DN34 8 B5
Normandy Rd. DN35 10 B4
Norsefield Av. DN37 16 C4
North Prom. DN35 10 C2
North Quay. DN31 9 G1
North Sea La. DN36 18 D1
North St. DN35 10 D4
Northumberland Clo. DN34 14 C1
Norwich Av. DN34 14 B2
Nunnerly Pl. DN37 16 D4
Nursery Gdns. DN36 19 F5
Oak Av. DN32 15 E3
Oak Rd. DN37 6 C2
Oak Way. DN35 11 B7
Oakwood Dri. DN37 7 E6
Oderin Dri. DN36 17 H2
Odin Ct. DN33 14 C4
Old Chapel La. DN37 12 B5
Old Farm Ct. DN37 16 A5
Old Fleet. DN37 7 E6
Old Market Pl. DN31 4 B3
Old Rd. DN37 7 E4
Oliver Ct. DN31 4 A1
Oliver St. DN35 10 B2
Oole Rd. DN35 10 D4
Orby Gro. DN33 14 A3
Orchard Ct. DN37 16 B5
Orchards Croft. DN33 16 D2
Orion Way. DN34 13 F2
Ormsby Clo. DN35 11 B6
Orwell St. DN31 9 F3
Osborne Dri. DN36 19 G6
Osborne St. DN31 4 C3
Osbourne St. DN35 10 D3
Oslear Cres. DN35 10 C4
Oxcombe Clo. DN33 16 B2
Oxford St, Cleethorpes. DN35 10 D4
Oxford St, Grimsby. DN32 9 G3

Pagehall Clo. DN33 14 D5
Paignton Ct. DN33 16 C3
Park Av. DN32 15 E2
Park Dri. DN32 14 D1
Park La. DN35 11 D8
Park St. DN35 9 H4
Park Vw. DN35 10 A2
Parker Rd. DN36 19 E2
Parker St. DN35 11 D5
Parris Pl. DN35 10 B3
Pasture St. DN31 4 C3
Patchett Clo. DN33 14 B5
Patrick St. DN32 15 E1
Paul Cres. DN36 18 D2
Peace Haven. DN37 16 B4
Peaks Av. DN36 17 G2
Peaks Field Av. DN32 15 E1
Peaks La. DN32 15 F2
Peaks La. DN36 17 H3
Peaks Parkway. DN32 4 D3
Pearson Rd. DN35 11 D6
Pelham Av. DN33 14 C
Pelham Pl. DN33 14 C
Pelham Rd, Cleethorpes. DN35 10 C
Pelham Rd, Grimsby. DN34 8 C
Pelham Rd, Holton le Clay. DN36 19 E
Pelham Sq. DN35 10 C
Pemberton Dri. DN36 17 F
Pembroke Av. DN34 8 A
Pembroke Rd. DN34 14 A
Pendeen Clo. DN36 17 G
Pendreth Pl. DN35 10 B
Penshurst Rd. DN35 11 B
Pepper Corn Wk. DN32 4 C
Peppercorn Wk. DN36 19 F
Perkins Clo. DN37 7 H
Pershore Av. DN34 13 F
Petchell Way. DN32 4 E
Peterhouse Rd. DN34 14 A
Phelps Pl. DN32 10 A
Phelps St. DN35 10 A
Philip Av. DN35 11 B
Philip Av. DN37 16 C
Philip Gro. DN35 11 B
Phillips La. DN37 12 B
Phoenix St. DN32 4 C
Phyllis Av. DN34 8 C
Phyllis Taylors Gdns. DN32 4 C
Piccadilly. DN36 17 G
Picksley Cres. DN36 19 F
Pine Clo. DN37 7 G
Pine Ct. DN35 11 B
Pine Wk. DN37 6 C
Pinewood Cres. DN33 14 A
Pinfold Gdns. DN36 19 G
Pinfold La, Holton le Clay. DN36 19 F
Pinfold La, Scartho. DN33 14 D
Pinneys Ct. DN37 6 B
Poplar Dri. DN36 19 F
Poplar Gro. DN35 10 C
Poplar Rd, Cleethorpes. DN35 10 C
Poplar Rd, Healing. DN37 6 B
Portland Av. DN32 15 E
Portland Pl. DN32 15 E
Pretymen Cres. DN36 17 G
Primrose Way. DN35 11 C8
Princes Rd. DN35 10 C
Princess Av. DN31 4 A
Priors Clo. DN36 17 H
Priory Rd. DN37 7 F6
Prystie Pl. DN35 11 B7
Purbeck Rd. DN33 16 C1
Pyewipe Rd. DN31 8 C4
Pytchley Wk. DN35 11 C7
Quantock Rd. DN33 16 C1
Queen Elizabeth Rd. DN36 18 D2
Queen Mary Av. DN35 10 A2
Queen St. DN31 4 D3
Queens Ct. DN34 14 A1
Queens Par, Cleethorpes. DN35 11 D5
Queens Par, Grimsby. DN31 4 A3
Queensway. DN37 7 G4
Quorn Mews. DN35 11 C7
Quinton Rd. DN32 15 E2

Radcliffe Rd. DN37 6 C3
Railway Pl. DN31 9 F3
Railway St. DN32 4 E1
Railway Ter. DN32 4 C4
Raithby Gro. DN33 14 A4
Ravendale Clo. DN36 19 G6
Ravendale Rd. DN35 11 E6
Ravenhill Clo. DN35 11 B6
Ravensburn St. DN31 4 A1
Ravensburn Way. DN31 4 A2
Ravenscar Rd. DN37 7 G4
Recto Av. DN32 15 F2
Redbourne Rd. DN33 14 B4
Redcar Gro. DN32 15 G2
Redwood Dri. DN35 11 B7
Regent Gdns. DN34 14 D1
Remillo Av. DN32 15 F2
Rendell St. DN31 8 D4
Reporto Av. DN32 15 F2
Responso Av. DN32 15 F2
Reston Ct. DN35 11 E6

eston Gro. DN33 14 B3
evesby Av. DN34 13 H3
evigo Av. DN32 15 F2
eynolds St. DN35 10 B3
ialto Av. DN32 15 F2
iby Ct. DN36 19 G5
iby Sq. DN31 9 F3
iby St. DN31 9 F3
ichard St. DN31 8 C4
ichardson Clo. DN36 19 E3
ichmond Rd. DN34 8 B6
ichmond Rd. DN35 11 C5
ipon St. DN31 8 C5
ivan Av. DN33 16 C2
ivan Gro. DN33 16 C2
iverside Dri. DN35 19 F1
oberts St. DN32 9 F5
obinson La. DN31 9 H3
obinson St East. DN32 4 D3
obson Rd. DN35 10 B3
ochester Ct. DN35 11 E8
ockingham Ct. DN34 13 F3
omsey Ct. DN34 13 F2
ookery Av. DN33 14 D3
ookery Rd. DN37 6 B3
opery St. DN32 4 F4
osaire Pl. DN33 17 E1
osalind Av. DN34 8 C5
osedale. DN37 16 B4
osemary Av. DN34 13 H1
osemary Way. DN35 11 C8
oseveare Av. DN34 8 B5
osina Gro Nth. DN32 9 H6
osina Gro Sth. DN32 9 H6
oss Rd. DN31 9 G3
othwell Av. DN33 14 B4
oundway. DN34 14 C2
owan Dri,
Healing. DN37 6 B2
owan Dri,
Humberston. DN36 19 E2
owston St. DN35 10 E4
oyal Ct. DN35 19 F1
oyal St. DN31 9 E3
udham Av. DN32 15 E3
ufford Rd. DN35 11 C5
unswick Rd. DN32 9 G6
ussell Ct. DN35 11 E8
utland Ct. DN32 9 G5
utland Dri. DN36 17 G4
utland St. DN32 9 G5
ydal Av. DN33 16 C2

ackville St. DN34 8 C6
agefield Clo. DN33 16 B1
t Albans Av. DN31 8 B5
t Andrews Dri. DN32 15 H2
t Andrews Rd. DN36 19 E2
t Anns Av. DN34 8 C6
t Augustine Av. DN32 15 E2
t Catherines Ct. DN34 13 H1
t Chads Gate. DN37 7 G4
t Chads Wk Sth. DN37 7 G4
t Clements Way.
DN36 17 G2
t Christophers Rd.
DN36 18 D2
t Edmunds Ct. DN34 13 H1
t Francis Av. DN31 8 B5
t Francis Gro. DN37 12 A5
t Giles Avenue. DN33 14 D6
t Helens Av. DN33 14 D3
t Heliers Rd. DN35 10 C3
t Hildas Av. DN34 8 C6
t Hughs Av. DN35 10 C4
t Ives Cres. DN34 13 G2
t James Av. DN34 8 A6
t James Ct. DN34 8 C6
t James Sq. DN31 4 B4
t Johns Ct. DN34 14 A1
t Johns Rd. DN36 18 D2
t Leonards Av. DN31 8 B4
t Lukes Ct. DN32 4 F2
t Lukes Cres. DN36 18 D2
t Margarets Clo. DN37 12 A5
t Marks Rd. DN36 18 D2
t Martins Cres. DN33 14 D3
t Marys Clo. DN32 10 A4
t Mathews Rd. DN36 18 D2
t Mawes Cres. DN34 8 A5
t Michaels Rd. DN34 13 G2
t Nicholas Dri. DN37 7 E6
t Olafs Gro. DN32 9 E6
t Peters Av. DN35 10 C3
t Peters Clo. DN36 19 F5
t Peters Cres. DN36 18 D2
St Peters Gro. DN37 12 A5
St Thomas Clo. DN36 18 D3
Salamander Clo. DN31 8 C4
Salisbury Av,
Grimsby. DN34 8 B6
Salisbury Av,
Waltham. DN37 16 B5
Salisbury Dri. DN37 16 B5
Salmeston Ct. DN34 8 C6
Saltburn Gro. DN32 15 G2
Saltgate. DN37 7 G4
Salvesen Rd. DN31 9 H3
Samuel Av. DN32 9 H6
Sanctuary Way. DN37 7 E6
Sanders St. DN31 8 C5
Sandford St. DN31 8 C4
Sandringham Rd. DN35 11 B5
Sarge Clo. DN336 19 F5
Sargon Way. DN37 7 H2
Saunby Gro. DN35 10 C3
Savoy Ct. DN36 17 G3
Saxby Gro. DN33 14 A3
Saxon Ct. DN31 8 B2
Saxon Cres. DN35 10 C4
Scampton Clo. DN34 14 B2
Scartho Rd. DN33 14 D3
Scawby Rd. DN33 14 A4
School Wk. DN35 11 A5
Scott Clo. DN37 7 H4
Scrivelsby Ct. DN35 11 E7
Sea Rd. DN35 10 D3
Sea View St. DN35 10 D4
Seacroft Rd. DN35 11 E5
Seaford Rd. DN35 19 E1
Seamer Gro. DN32 15 G1
Seaton Gro. DN32 15 G2
Second Av. DN33 14 C2
Seed Close La. DN37 12 B5
Segmere St. DN35 10 E4
Selbourne Rd. DN34 13 G3
Selge Way. DN33 14 A4
Selwyn Ct. DN34 13 H1
Service Rd 1. DN37 7 G4
Service Rd 2. DN37 7 G4
Service Rd 3. DN37 7 G4
Service Rd 4. DN37 7 G4
Service Rd 5. DN37 7 G4
Service Rd 6. DN37 7 H4
Service Rd 7. DN37 7 H4
Service Rd 8. DN37 7 G4
Service Rd 9. DN37 7 G4
Service Rd 10. DN37 7 G4
Service Rd 11. DN37 7 G4
Service Rd 12. DN37 7 G3
Service Rd 13. DN37 7 G3
Service Rd 15. DN37 7 G4
Service Rd 16. DN37 7 G4
Service Rd 17. DN37 7 H4
Service Rd 18. DN37 7 H4
Service Rd 19. DN37 7 H4
Service Rd 20. DN37 7 H5
Service Rd 21. DN37 7 G4
Service Rd 22. DN37 7 G4
Service Rd 23. DN37 7 G4
Service Rd 26. DN37 7 G4
Severn Way. DN37 7 G4
Shaftesbury Mews.
DN36 17 G3
Shaw Dri. DN33 17 E1
Shears Ct. DN37 16 D5
Sheepfold St. DN32 4 D3
Shelley Av. DN33 14 B3
Sheraton Dri. DN36 18 D2
Sherburn St. DN35 11 C5
Sherwood Rd. DN34 13 G2
Side La. DN33 17 E2
Sidney Pl. DN35 9 H4
Sidney Rd. DN34 8 B5
Sidney St. DN35 9 H4
Sidney Taylor Wk.
DN36 17 G2
Sidney Way, DN35 9 H4
Signhills Av. DN35 11 E5
Silver St,
Grimsby. DN31 4 B3
Silver St,
Holton le Clay. DN36 19 F6
Silvergarth. DN32 15 G2
Simons Pl. DN35 10 B3
Sinderson Rd. DN36 19 E2
Sixhills St. DN32 4 D3
Skinners La. DN37 16 C5
Snowdrop Clo. DN37 6 B3
Solomon Ct. DN35 11 B5
Somersby St. DN31 4 B2
Sophia Av. DN33 14 C6
South Parade. DN31 4 B2
South Sea La. DN36 18 D4
South St Marys Gate.
DN31 4 B3
South St. DN35 10 E4
South Vw,
Grimbsy. DN34 8 A6
South Vw,
Holton le Clay. DN36 19 G6
South Vw,
Humberston. DN36 18 D2
Southern Wk. DN33 16 D2
Southfield Av. DN33 16 D2
Southfield Rd,
Holton le Clay. DN36 19 F6
Southfield Rd,
Scartho. DN33 16 D2
Southland Way. DN37 7 H4
Southwold Cres. DN33 16 C1
Sovereign Clo. DN34 13 F3
Spark St. DN34 8 B5
Spencer St. DN31 9 H3
Spring Bank. DN34 8 A5
Spring La. DN37 12 B5
Springfield Rd. DN33 16 B1
Springway Cres. DN34 8 A5
Springwood Cres.
DN33 16 B2
Spurn Av. DN33 16 D1
Stainton Av. DN33 14 A3
Stallingborough Rd.
DN37 6 A2
Stanford Clo. DN37 12 B4
Stanhope Pl. DN35 10 A3
Stanland Way. DN36 18 D2
Stanley St. DN32 9 G5
Station Av. DN36 17 G3
Station Rd,
Cleethorpes. DN35 10 D3
Station Rd,
Great Coates. DN37 7 F4
Station Rd,
Healing. DN37 6 B3
Station Rd,
New Waltham. DN36 17 F3
Station Rd,
Waltham. DN37 16 D4
Stephen Cres,
Humberston. DN36 18 D2
Stephen Cres,
Laceby Acres. DN34 13 G3
Sterling Cres. DN37 16 A6
Stevenson Pl. DN35 10 B4
Stirling St. DN31 9 G3
Stokesley Wk. DN37 7 H4
Stortford St. DN31 8 B3
Stow Clo. DN37 7 F4
Strand St. DN32 9 F3
Strange Wk. DN36 18 D2
Stratford Av. DN33 14 A3
Stratton Ct. DN34 13 E2
Strawberry Hill. DN37 16 A5
Strubby Clo. DN35 11 E6
Stuart Wortley St. DN31 9 F2
Sturton Gro. DN33 14 B3
Suggitts Ct. DN35 10 B2
Suggitts La. DN35 10 B2
Suggitts Orchard. DN35 10 C2
Summerfield Av. DN37 16 C4
Summerfield Clo. DN37 16 C4
Sunningdale. DN37 16 A5
Sunny Cnr. DN33 14 D5
Surtees St. DN31 9 F2
Sussex St. DN35 9 H4
Sutcliffe Av. DN33 14 A3
Swaby Dri. DN35 11 B6
Swales Rd. DN36 19 E2
Swallow Dri. DN37 6 B3
Sweetbriar Clo. DN37 16 A4
Swiftsure Cres. DN34 13 F2
Swinderby Gdns. DN34 14 A2
Sycamore Av. DN33 14 D4

Tallert Way. DN33 13 H4
Tamar Dri. DN36 17 H2
Tasburgh. DN32 9 F6
Tattershall Av. DN34 13 H3
Taunton Way. DN33 16 D1
Taylor St. DN35 9 H3
Taylors Av. DN35 11 B7
Tealby Gro. DN33 14 B3
Team Gate. DN37 7 E6
Telford Pl. DN34 8 A5
Tenby Wk. DN34 8 B5
Tennyson Mews. DN31 4 B1
Tennyson Rd. DN35 10 C3
Tennyson St. DN31 4 B1
Terrington Pl. DN35 11 B5
Tetney La. DN36 19 G5
Tetney Rd. DN36 18 D3
Tewkesbury Ct. DN34 8 C6
The Avenue,
Great Coates. DN37 7 F4
The Avenue,
Healing. DN37 6 B3
The Berea. DN34 14 C2
The Cloisters,
Great Coates. DN37 7 F6
The Cloisters,
Humberston. DN36 19 E3
The Close. DN34 8 C6
The Copse. DN33 16 D1
The Crescent. DN36 19 E5
The Crest. DN34 14 C2
The Crofts. DN36 18 D2
The Crossway. DN34 13 G3
The Drawing Ct. DN31 8 B2
The Drive. DN37 16 D6
The Elms. DN36 18 D3
The Gathering. DN35 10 C4
The Lanes. DN34 8 C6
The Mead. DN37 12 B5
The Orchard. DN36 17 G3
The Oval. DN33 14 C5
The Ridgeway. DN34 13 F3
The Smooting. DN36 19 F5
The Spinney. DN34 8 C6
The Square. DN32 9 G4
Thesiger St. DN32 9 F4
Thirkleby Cres. DN32 15 G2
Thirlmere Av. DN33 16 C2
Thomas St. DN32 4 F3
Thoresby Pl. DN35 11 C6
Thoresway Gro. DN33 14 A4
Thorganby Rd. DN35 11 E6
Thornhill Gdns. DN34 8 A5
Thornton Ct. DN36 17 G2
Thornton Cres. DN35 11 C5
Thornton Gro. DN34 13 G3
Thorold St. DN31 9 G3
Thrunscoe Rd. DN35 11 D5
Timberley Dri. DN37 7 F5
Tintagel Way. DN36 17 G2
Tintern Wk. DN37 7 G3
Tiverton St. DN35 10 A2
Toll Bar Av. DN36 17 F3
Tom Hammond Way.
DN32 9 F4
Tomline St. DN31 9 F3
Tonbridge Wk. DN33 16 C1
Tonnant Way. DN34 13 F2
Toothill Gdns. DN34 7 H6
Toothill Rd. DN34 7 H6
Torbay Dri. DN33 16 C3
Torksey Dri. DN33 14 B3
Torrington St. DN32 15 F1
Totnes Rd. DN33 16 C3
Town Hall Sq. DN31 4 C3
Town Hall St. DN31 4 C3
Townsend Clo. DN36 19 F1
Toynton Pl. DN33 14 B4
Toynton Rd. DN33 14 B3
*Toynton Wk,
Toynton Rd. DN33 14 B4
Trafalgar Av. DN34 13 F2
Trafalgar Pk. DN36 17 H2
Tranby Dri. DN32 15 H2
Trevor Clo. DN37 12 B5
Trinity Rd. DN35 11 C5
Trinity St. DN31 9 G3
Tunnard St. DN32 9 G4
Turnberry App. DN37 16 B5
Twyning Pl. DN35 10 B2
Tyler Av. DN31 8 B5
Tyne Way. DN37 7 G4

Ulster Av. DN33 14 D4
Unity Rd. DN32 10 A4
Upper Burgess St. DN31 4 D2
Upper Burgess St. DN31 4 D3
Upper Spring St. DN31 4 D2
Utgard Way. DN33 14 B4
Utterby Dri. DN34 14 C1

Vaughan Av. DN32 15 H2
Veal St. DN31 8 C5
Vicarage Gdns. DN34 8 C6
Vicarage Lawn. DN34 8 C6
Victor St. DN32 9 G3
Victoria Ct. DN31 4 C1
Victoria St Nth. DN31 4 C1
Victoria St Sth. DN31 4 C1
Victoria St West. DN31 4 B3
Victory Way. DN34 13 F3
Violet Clo. DN35 11 C8
Viscount Way. DN36 19 F2
Vivian Av. DN32 15 H2

Waby Clo. DN37 7 F4
Waddingham Pl. DN36 17 H4
Waddington Pl. DN34 14 A2
Waldorf Rd. DN35 11 E8
WalesbyClo. DN33 16 B2
Walk La. DN36 18 D4
Walker Av. DN33 16 D1
Wall St. DN34 8 B5
Walmsgate. DN33 14 B3
Walmsgate Pl. DN33 14 B3
Walnut Cres. DN35 11 B7
Walsh Gdns. DN33 14 B5
Waltham Rd. DN33 16 D1
Walton Gro. DN33 14 C3
Ward St. DN35 10 A2
Wardall St. DN35 10 D4
Warneford Rd. DN35 10 B2
Warwick Av. DN33 14 A3
Warwick Rd. DN35 11 B5
Waterloo Dri. DN33 14 C5
Waterside Dri. DN31 4 A2
Watford Av. DN34 14 A2
Watkin St Nth. DN31 8 D4
Watkin St Sth. DN31 8 D4
Wayside Clo. DN36 19 G5
Wayside Dri. DN36 17 G2
Weekes Rd. DN35 11 D6
Weelsby Av. DN32 15 E2
Weelsby Gro. DN32 15 E2
Weelsby Rd. DN32 14 D2
Weelsby St. DN32 9 G5
Weelsby St Sth. DN32 9 G5
Weelsby Vw. DN36 17 H1
Welbeck Pl. DN34 13 H2
Welbeck Rd,
Cleethorpes. DN35 11 A5
Welbeck Rd,
Laceby Acres. DN34 13 G2
Welholme Av. DN32 14 D1
Welholme Rd. DN32 14 D1
Well Vale. DN33 16 C1
Welland Av. DN34 13 H2
Wellgarth. DN32 15 G2
Wellington St. DN32 4 E2
Wellowgate DN32 4 B4
Wellowgate Mews.
DN32 4 B4
Wells Cres. DN35 11 C7
Wells Rd. DN37 6 A3
Wells St. DN31 8 C5
Wendover Clo. DN36 19 E3
Wendover Rise. DN35 11 D5
Wentworth Rd. DN34 8 B5
Werneth Rd. DN32 4 E2
Wesley Cres. DN35 11 C6
West Coates Rd. DN31 8 C3
West Lea. DN33 16 D2
West St Marys Gate.
DN31 4 B3
West St. DN35 10 D4
Westbourne Gro.
DN33 16 D2
Westbury Pk. DN35 11 E8
Westbury Rd. DN35 11 E8
Westerdale Way. DN37 7 G4
Western Outway. DN34 14 A2
Westfield Av. DN33 14 D3
Westfield Gro. DN35 10 B4
Westfield Rd. DN37 16 B5
Westgate. DN31 8 D3
Westhill Rd. DN34 14 B1
Westkirke Av. DN33 17 E1
Westlands Av. DN34 14 C1
Westminster Dri. DN34 8 C6
Westport Rd. DN35 11 E8
Westside Rd. DN31 8 C2
Westward Clo. DN34 14 C2
Westward Ho. DN34 14 B1
Westwood Rd. DN37 6 B2
Weyford Rd. DN35 11 E8
Wharfedale Way. DN31 4 B1
Wharncliffe Rd Nth.
DN31 9 F1
Wharton St. DN31 8 C5
Wheatfield Dri. DN37 16 A5
Whernside Wk. DN31 4 B2
Whimbrel Way. DN36 17 H2
Whisby Ct. DN36 19 G5
Whitby Dri. DN32 15 G2

Whitehall Country Cotts. DN35 11 E8
Whitehall Rd. DN35 11 E8
Whites Rd. DN35 11 D5
Whitgift Clo. DN37 12 B5
Whitgift Way. DN37 7 G4
Wickenby Clo. DN34 13 H2
Wickham Rd. DN31 9 G3
Wicklow Av. DN33 16 C1
William St. DN35 10 D4
Willing Way. DN32 4 F2
Willingham St. DN32 4 D4
Willoughby Gro. DN34 13 H2
Willow Clo. DN37 12 A5
Wilson St. DN35 10 B2
Wilton Rd. DN36 18 B1
Wimborn Av. DN34 8 B6
Winceby Av. DN31 8 B5
Winchcombe Av. DN34 13 G2
Winchester Av. DN33 14 A3
Windermere Av. DN33 16 C2
Windermere Cres. DN36 18 C1
Windlesham Av. DN33 16 B2
Windsor Rd. DN35 11 A5
Wingate Par. DN37 7 G4
Wingate Rd. DN37 7 F4
Winn Ct. DN35 10 C4
Winslow Gro. DN34 14 A2
Winston Av. DN34 8 B6
Winthorpe Rd. DN33 14 C4
Wintringham Rd. DN32 9 E6
Wirral Av. DN34 13 H2
Wisteria Dri. DN37 6 A3
Withern Rd. DN33 14 A4
Woad La. DN37 7 G3
Wold View. DN36 19 F5
Wollaston Rd. DN35 10 C4
Womersley Rd. DN31 9 G3
Wood Clo. DN33 16 D2
Wood St. DN32 4 E1
Woodfield Clo. DN36 18 D2
Woodhall Dri. DN37 16 A5
Woodland Wk. DN35 11 C8
Woodrow Pk. DN33 14 D5
Woodsley Av. DN35 11 C5
Wootton Rd. DN33 14 B3
Worcester Av. DN34 14 A2
Worlaby Rd. DN33 16 B1
Worsley Clo. DN36 19 F5
Wragby St. DN32 4 F3
Wray Clo. DN37 16 A5
Wren Clo. DN37 6 B3
Wren Cres. DN33 14 C4
Wroxham Av. DN34 13 G2
Wybers Way. DN37 7 F5
Wymark Vw. DN33 14 A4
Wyndham Rd. DN36 17 G3

Yarborough Dri. DN31 4 A2
Yarborough Rd. DN34 8 A6
Yardley Way. DN34 13 F2
Yarorough Clo. DN36 19 F5
Yarra Rd. DN35 10 D4
Yarrow Rd. DN34 7 G6
Yew's La. DN37 12 A5
York Pl. DN35 11 A5
York St. DN31 4 A1
Young Pl. DN35 9 H5

IMMINGHAM

Ainsworth Rd. DN40 5 B2
Aire Clo. DN40 5 B3
Alden Clo. DN40 5 C2
Alderney Way. DN40 5 C4
Allerton Dri. DN40 5 C2
Ancholme Av. DN40 5 A3
Anglesey Dri. DN40 5 C4
Arran Clo. DN40 5 D4
Ash Tree Clo. DN40 5 C1
Atwood Clo. DN40 5 B1
Balfour Pl. DN40 5 B2
Barnard Wk. DN40 5 D3
Battery St. DN40 5 D2
Beechwood Av. DN40 5 C2
Birkdale Dri. DN40 5 D1
Blair Wk. DN40 5 E3
Blossom Way. DN40 5 B3
Bluestone La. DN40 5 B2
Bowman Way. DN40 5 B3
Bradford Rd. DN40 5 B2
Brewster Av. DN40 5 D3
Calder Clo. DN40 5 A3
Carver Rd. DN40 5 D3
Cedar Dri. DN40 5 C1
Chestnut Av. DN40 5 E1
Chilton Clo. DN40 5 B2
Church La. DN40 5 B1
Clarence Clo. DN40 5 B3
Cleveland Clo. DN40 5 A2
Clyfton Cres. DN40 5 B2
Collier Rd. DN40 5 D3
Copse Clo. DN40 5 C1
Corfe Wk. DN40 5 E3
Craik Hill Av. DN40 5 C3
Cushman Cres. DN40 5 C3
Deane Rd. DN40 5 D2
Dunster Wk. DN40 5 E3
Eaton Rd. DN40 5 D2
Fairisle Rise. DN40 5 D4
Ferndown Dri. DN40 5 D1
Green La. DN40 5 B2
Guernsey Gro. DN40 5 C4
Habrough Rd. DN40 5 A3
Hadleigh Rd. DN40 5 D3
Hamish Wk. DN40 5 B3
Harlech Wk. DN40 5 D3
Hawthorn Av. DN40 5 E1
Hazel Croft. DN40 5 A2
Helen Cres. DN40 5 A2
Highfield Av. DN40 5 B3
Highland Tarn. DN40 5 B3
Hinkley Dri. DN40 5 B1
Holbeck Pl. DN40 5 B2
Hollingsworth Av. DN40 5 B2
Hoylake Dri. DN40 5 D1
Humberville Rd. DN40 5 D2
Hume Brae. DN40 5 B3
INDUSTRIAL & RETAIL:
Pelham Ind Est. DN40 5 D1
Ings La. DN40 5 D2
Jackson Mews. DN40 5 A2
James Way. DN40 5 B3
Japonica Hill. DN40 5 C3
Jasmine Way. DN40 5 C3
Kendal Rd. DN40 5 E3
Kings Rd. DN40 5 E1
Kinloch Way. DN40 5 B3
Kishorn Ct. DN40 5 B3
Langley Wk. DN40 5 D3
Lansdown Rd. DN40 5 B2
Larch Clo. DN40 5 E1
Leyden Clo. DN40 5 B2
Lindum Av. DN40 5 B3
Lulworth Wk. DN40 5 D3
Lundy Ct. DN40 5 C4
Lydford Rd. DN40 5 D3
Lydia Ct. DN40 5 A2
Magnolia Rise. DN40 5 C3
Maiden Clo. DN40 5 A2
Manby Rd. DN40 5 D1
Maple Gro. DN40 5 C1
Margaret St. DN40 5 C2
Mayflower Av. DN40 5 C3
McKenzie Pl. DN40 5 B3
Middleplatt Rd. DN40 5 E1
Mill La. DN40 5 A2
Millhouse Rise. DN40 5 A2
Morton Clo. DN40 5 B2
Muirfield Ct. DN40 5 D2
Muirfield Croft. DN40 5 D2
Mull Way. DN40 5 C4
Newark Wk. DN40 5 D3
Newport Wk. DN40 5 D3
Oakham Wk. DN40 5 E3
Oaklands Rd. DN40 5 C1
Oban Ct. DN40 5 B3
Orkney Pl. DN40 5 D3
Paddock Ct. DN40 5 C
Pamela Clo. DN40 5 D
Pamela Rd. DN40 5 D
Park Clo. DN40 5 C
Pelham Rd. DN40 5 E
Pennine Clo. DN40 5 A
Perth Way. DN40 5 B
Pilgrim Av. DN40 5 C
Pilgrims Way. DN40 5 A
Princess St. DN40 5 C
Robert Clo. DN40 5 E
Rose Gdns. DN40 5 C
Roundway. DN40 5 C
Roval Dri. DN40 5 A
Sackville Clo. DN40 5 D
Sackville Rd. DN40 5 D
St Andrews La. DN40 5 B
St Andrews Way. DN40 5 A
Shetland Way. DN40 5 C
Somerton Rd. DN40 5 E
Sonia Crest. DN40 5 B
Spinney Clo. DN40 5 C
Spring St. DN40 5 D
Stainton Dri. DN40 5 B
Stallingborough Rd. DN40 5 B
Standish La. DN40 5 B
Steeping Dri. DN40 5 A
Sunningdale Dri. DN40 5 D
Talbot Rd. DN40 5 D
Thornbury Rd. DN40 5 D
Thornton Pl. DN40 5 C
Trenchard Clo. DN40 5 E
Tummel Ct. DN40 5 B
Valda Vale. DN40 5 B
Viking Clo. DN40 5 A
Washdyke La. DN40 5 C
Waterworks St. DN40 5 E
Weston Gro. DN40 5 B
Winslow Dri. DN40 5 B
Woodlands Av. DN40 5 C
Worsley Clo. DN40 5 D
Worsley Rd. DN40 5 D

Edition 538 C 01.01.